The Perfect Piggy

Joanne Rowe

The Perfect Piggy

A guide to keeping Teacup Pigs, Micro Pigs and other Pet Pigs

The Perfect Piggy

ISBN-13: 978-1494824501

ISBN-10: 1494824507

Book Website: Lancashiremicropigs.co.uk

Email: info@Lancashiremicropigs.co.uk

Give feedback on the book at:

- http://www.amazon.com/dp/B00H52F4KW - USA Link
- https://www.amazon.co.uk/dp/B00H52F4KW - UK Link
- info@Lancashiremicropigs.co.uk
- Printed internationally using CreateSpace

"I am fond of pigs. Dogs look up to us. Cats look down on us. Pigs treat us as equals." - Winston Churchill

Disclaimer:

This book is not intended as a substitute for the medical advice of veterinarians. The reader should regularly consult a veterinarian in matters relating to their pig's health and particularly with respect to any symptoms that may require diagnosis or medical attention.

This book is presented solely for educational and entertainment purposes. The author and publisher are not offering it as legal, medical, veterinary, or other professional services advice. Neither the publisher nor the individual author(s) shall be liable for any physical, psychological, emotional, financial, or commercial damages, including, but not limited to, special, incidental, consequential or other damages. Our views and rights are the same: You are responsible for your own choices, actions, and results.

Contents

Glossary

Here is an explanation of some of the technical terms used throughout the book:

Sow – Female pig.

Gilt – Female pig. This term is applied to them just before they farrow.

Boar – Uncastrated male pig.

Barrow – Castrated male pig.

Swine – Another word for pigs.

Farrowing – Giving birth.

Vulva – External parts of the sow's genitals.

Sow Nuts – Dry feed designed for pigs, usually comes in pellet form.

Hogging – Also known as 'monthly cycle', 'come into heat', 'heats' or 'in season'. This is the oestrous cycle of a sow.

Hogs – Another term used for pigs but it usually means the domestic farm breeds reared for meat

Introduction

This book originally started out as a short, seven-page care guide that we used to give to people who bought Micro Pigs from our farm in Lancashire, England.

Our little guide simply outlined the basics of Micro Pig care, and ensured that the new owners got off to the best possible start. Our original guide was a real success and many of our customers found it really helpful.

One day we decided expand on the things in the guide, we thought we'd try and write everything we knew about pet pigs and Micro Pigs. The result is the book you are reading now.

We've learnt a lot in the years that we have been keeping and breeding these types of pigs, and we want to pass on the benefit of our experience to any new, or existing, owners.

The aim of this guide is to give you lots of practical hints and tips. If you follow our advice you and your new pet will get off to a great start.

This book has been written primarily for British and American owners. Unlike other books we will cover the laws concerning pigs in their respective countries. We also offer some general advice for those folk who live in other countries.

Chapter 1 - Breeds of Pet Pigs

Photo above: A Micro Piglet

The British Micro Pig

The origins of the British Micro Pig can be traced back to Cumbria, England. In 1995, a man named Rob Rose (www.valleyofthepigs.co.uk) was the first person in the UK to create the first generation of the breed we now call 'Micro Pigs'.

The first generation of Micro Pigs were much larger than the pigs you see today. Rob achieved these sizes through selectively breeding the smallest and fittest animals with each other. Slowly, overtime, he managed to reduce the adult sizes of these pigs, eventually resulting in the Micro Pigs we see today.

Selective breeding is commonly used in the farming industry, and has been for hundreds of years. Generally the desired traits in pigs have been for a bigger animal with more meat, fat, and weight, with the Micro Pig the process was simply reversed.

The actual British Micro Pig (and other worldwide equivalents) is a hybrid; it's the result of crossbreeding various standard breeds with miniature Potbellied pigs. The purpose of this crossbreeding was to produce a small pig, in a variety of colours, with a good temperament.

Another misconception about these pigs is that the New Zealand Kune Kune was used in the breeding of the British Micro Pig. This is not true; the Kune Kune should never be used in the breeding of these pigs. If you come across pigs which have been bred with Kune Kunes then these pigs are not true British Micro Pigs. Be wary of breeders making such claims.

There are other breeders around the world who have achieved the same result via a different path. In the US, the Royal Dandy is another breed famous for being a small pet pig. I've also heard of several other Micro Pig breeds in Europe and other parts of the world.

There has always been a demand for a small pig which makes a great pet. It should come as no surprise that various breeders around the globe have come up with their own solutions to fulfil this demand. Who came first? Well, no one knows. Some breeders have kept records, some haven't. With no official global regulator, or pedigree system, no one can actually be sure. Personally, I don't think it matters much when buying a pet pig, there are far more important things to consider. One thing we have always told people about these pigs is that the size of them doesn't make them easier or harder to care for–it's all about how you keep them: and that's the basis of this book.

The Shape of Micro Pigs

One thing to bear in mind about these animals is their shape. As mentioned earlier the Micro Pig is a hybrid–it's a mixture of pig breeds–so their shape can vary.

Some Micro Pigs can be closer to their original Potbellied ancestors; this can be evident in their shape and stature. Black Micro Pigs are the greatest example of this and bear the closest resemblance to their original Potbellied ancestors. The black piglets share a lot of features with their original Potbellied parents, including: a pug nose, a dish shaped face, and a prominent pot belly.

The black type piglets are often the smallest in height of the various different coloured varieties Micro Pigs due to their genes being more closely aligned with the common potbelly.

Other Micro Pigs, especially the coloured varieties (pinks, gingers, browns and any non-black pigs) have less of the Potbellied genes inside them and their shape will usually resemble their non-Potbellied forefathers. Various different breeds including Gloucester, Tamworth and Berkshire have been used in the breeding of micro pigs, and evidence of their genetic heritage can be seen in their shape.

The coloured Micro Pigs are usually taller than their black counterparts due to the introduction of non-Potbellied genes to their family history. The differences in height can vary greatly depending on which generation of pigs you are looking at. However the coloured pigs can have the illusion of looking smaller due to their frame and girth being smaller. There is also the lack of the pug nose, and dish shaped face, that the potbelly is famous for.

Both types of pig do share the trait of having a straight tail. Any legitimate Micro Pig should have a straight tail (non-curly), this is an important feature to keep an eye out for when buying a Micro Pig. Curly tails can be an indication that you might be buying, or looking at, a domestic hog, so please beware.

The Kune Kune Pig

Kune Kune are a very popular pig from New Zealand. During the 19th century it was imported to New Zealand, from Asia, by whalers. The origins of the pig before this time are unclear.

In the early 1900s the pig grew in popularity with New Zealand's native Maori. In Maori the word Kune Kune means 'fat and round'. The Maori prized the pig due to its friendly nature, its tendency not to roam, and its great grazing ability (the pig could be fattened on grass alone).

During the mid-20th century the popularity of the pig dropped; modern commercial breeds were gaining recognition and were preferred for use in pork production. More traditional breeds like the Kune Kune were slowly made redundant by their more efficient cousins.

The breed was thought to be nearly extinct by the 1980s. There was estimated to be only around fifty purebred Kune Kune left in New Zealand. But thanks to the efforts of a handful of New Zealand breeders a recovery program was put in place that helped save the breed.

In the 1990s the breed was imported into the UK for the first time. Later, around the mid-90s, they were imported into the USA however it wasn't until after 2007 that the breed became more commercially available and widespread.

Kune Kune Appearance

The Kune Kune is famous for being a little hairy pig that comes in a wide range of colours and spots. Some pigs have straight or curly hair; others can have long or short hair. They can have various hair colours, including; cream, ginger, gold, white, tan, and black. The unique characteristic of a Kune Kune are the tassels (pire pire) which can be found hanging from their lower jaw. The shape of the Kune Kune is small and round, with short legs, and a short, up-turned snout.

The breed does vary in size, the smallest Kune Kunes are around 24 inches in height (measured from foot to shoulder), and the biggest are usually around 30 inches high. A fat Kune Kune can have the appearance of being bigger than these sizes though. A healthy Kune Kune should weigh between 60kg and 200 kg when fully grown (pigs are usually fully grown between 3-5 years).

The Kune Kune as a Pet

Today the Kune Kune is more popular as ever. Worldwide there are now more breeders than ever before. These days you don't have to travel far before being able to see these pigs in person. Official breeder's clubs can now be found in various countries, dedicated to promoting an established standard. This involves recording the breeding of the pig, maintaining a pedigree system, and helping to promote good practice. These clubs also publish a yearly newsletter and run discussion forums. I believe this to be one of the Kune Kune's biggest advantages over the Micro Pig.

There are no breeding clubs for the Micro Pig in the USA, UK, or the rest of the world. There's no established standard for the breed; no family and genetic history is ever recorded; and there are no official Micro Pig clubs or pedigree systems in place. These are just some of the reasons why the Micro Pig is criticised by other breeders.

A Kune Kune can make a great pet. They're small, friendly and enjoy the company of humans. They're not prone to wandering and have a tendency not to root (pigs that root will annihilate a nice looking garden or paddock). With these great traits, and established clubs helping to support the breed, the Kune Kune is a serious alternative to a Micro Pig. To learn more about this wonderful, little, hairy pig check out the British Kune Kune Pig Society website:

http://www.britishkunekunesociety.org.uk/

Photo above: Potbelly pig

Photo above: Kune Kune piglets

Potbelly Pig

The potbelly has probably the longest and most well documented history out of all the common pet pigs. It's an Asian swine breed (known as Sus Scrofa in Latin) and is believed to be a descendant of the Chinese pigs that were domesticated around 10,000 years ago. Chinese pigs have a similar appearance and shape–they have perky ears, straight tails and a straight back.

Potbellied pigs were routinely kept by Vietnamese families to provide a regular source of food and fat as 50% of a potbelly pig's body is fat; whereas a modern farm pig's body fat is usually between 5-15%, depending on the breed.

Demand for pigs with large fat reserves has reduced steadily over the last sixty years; this has resulted in modern farm swine replacing the Potbellies in their home countries.

Modern farm pigs produce more meat, less fat, and are cheaper to raise. Today they have pretty much replaced their Potbellied cousins in their native countries: it's believed the original potbellies are practically extinct!

Sometime during the last 100 years the Potbellied pig was brought to Europe. In the mid-80s the first potbellies were shipped to Canada by a man named Connell, where they were destined to be used in lab experiments. Laboratories favoured the pig because of its small size when compared with common farm hogs. The original Potbellied pigs weighed approximately 200lbs (90 kg), most farm hogs can weigh upwards of 800lbs (362 kg). The small size of the potbelly made them far easier to keep and handle.

During the late 80s the first of these Connell pigs made their way into a zoo in the USA. The zoo bred these pigs and sold their offspring to the pet industry. This was the start of the first Potbellied pig craze.

During this time several other groups of smaller pigs were imported into the USA. Breeders also started cross-breeding their pigs with smaller farm hogs and feral pigs. Around this time the first registries were setup and they proceeded to track the imported pigs and their descendants.

Competitions and pig shows also sprang up during this period and top prize winning pigs were being sold for thousands of dollars. But it didn't continue. The fad quickly faded–the registries closed, the competitions stopped, and more and more Potbellied pigs ended up in sanctuaries or were simply abandoned.

As the years moved on the different blood lines were bred with each other. Almost all the Potbellied pigs in the USA today are a mix of these original lines. The different variations of potbelly pig (such as the Swedish White and Juliana) are thought to have been completely combined with the other potbelly breeding lines. It is thought that there are no pure bred lines of the Swedish White and Juliana pigs left in the USA today.

The only registry collecting data on these breeding lines closed in the mid-90s, so there is no way to accurately trace the ancestry of these pigs after that point. If you come across breeders in the US who claim to breed pure Juliana and Swedish White pigs their claims are likely to be false. Any legitimate breeder of these strains must have kept their own records since the closure of the original registry in the 90s, this would be only way to backup such claims.

Appearance of the Potbelly

The modern potbelly pig has many different variations. Most of the modern pigs are smaller than the original Connell lines. Some are quite tall, growing up to 26" in height, whilst others are on the smaller side (90-100lbs, around 16"-22" in height). The modern potbelly also comes in a variety of colours including: black, white with black/red spots, silver, or red. All of these coloured pigs are potbellies and are equally good as pets.

Potbellied Pigs in the UK

During the late 80s and 90s it is thought that various groups of people imported these pigs, and the other variations (Juliana and Swedish White), from Europe. However, due to the lack of a UK-based potbelly register, there is no way to trace the movement or the breeding of these pigs. Just like in the USA these pigs have been crossbred with other breeds to produce different variations.

Potbellied pigs make a great pet – it's friendly, enjoys the company of humans and has a tendency not to root. There are plenty of websites, books, and clubs all dedicated to the breed. Also, due to it being the first 'real' pet pig, there's more information about keeping them as pets than any other breed. The great thing is that this wealth of information and advice can be used to help your pet pig, regardless of its breed.

Other Types of Pig as Pets

The previous three breeds are the best pet-pig breeds and are ideal for the beginner. However, people do keep other breeds of pig as pets. I've heard of people in the USA, Australia, and other countries, keeping feral pigs as pets. A feral pig is a pig that's usually not a native breed, and is one that has gone wild. I've also heard about people keeping traditional farm hogs as pets. Keeping feral and traditional hogs as pets requires acres of land, robust fencing and a dedicated area or paddock setup for the pig–a place where the animal can cause damage without it being a problem. Traditional farm hogs can grow <u>very</u> large, depending on the breed; this reduces their suitability as a pet in a domestic setting.

Certain breeds, like the Gloucester Old Spot, are widely known as being a 'rooting' pig. These pigs are like a four-legged plough and can turn over a large area of land in a few days. Again, this sort of behaviour could be a problem for anyone who is planning on keeping them in a back garden, allotment or house.

If you have the land and space, and you don't mind owning a big pig, and rooting is not a problem, then there could be nothing stopping you from owning a farm hog as a pet. Pigs are pigs, they all share the same psychology, motivations, physiology, and are all food orientated individuals. They can all be kept as pets, but some breeds are far more suitable and easier to keep than others. I strongly recommend sticking to the Potbelly, Kune Kune, or a Micro Pig, when considering a pig as a pet. If you are thinking of buying a farm hog, then make sure you thoroughly researched the breed before you commit to anything. Certain farm breeds have particular quirks and unique characteristics that you should be aware of before you buy.

Which Breeds are Best: The Conclusion?

So, which pig is best? Well, it's up to you to decide. Like buying a car it's a matter of personal taste.

The Kune Kune and Potbellied pigs should definitely be on your viewing list when considering a pig as a pet. The existence of established registries for these breeds is a clear advantage. Breed registries usually hold a list of established breeders who adhere to the club's rules on breeding and care. Established pig clubs also make the task of finding a good breeder far easier–the clubs' websites are usually a fantastic source of information.

When buying Micro Pigs things are trickier. There is no established standard for the breed. There are no official clubs, or registries, or forums dedicated to the breed. This can make finding a good breeder extremely difficult. Finding breeders who can provide testimonials, and who are knowledgeable about the breed, is a good place to start.

Due to the high prices involved within the Micro Pig industry it has its fair share of rogue traders, back-yard breeders, and con artists selling these pigs. However, by reading this book, we hope to arm you with the knowledge to help you avoid the worst scams and the bad breeders.

Potbellies and Kune Kunes are not immune to bad breeders and mis-selling. However, due to the money involved in the Micro Pig industry they seem to be the pig that suffers the worst of these problems.

Chapter 2 - Micro Pig Size – How big do they grow?

Micro Pig Size and Height

I've decided to dedicate a whole chapter to Micro Pig size as this is the one area which causes the most confusion. By the end of this chapter you should have a clearer idea of just how big a Micro Pig actually is. I'll also show you a few common scams and how to avoid some the most frequent mistakes people make when considering a Micro Pig as pet.

How Big do they Grow...?

The most common question asked about the Micro Pig is: how big do they grow? These days you can find more information online about this subject than ever before, however, you'll still see a lot of conflicting opinions and advice.

Take this as a classic example: try using the Internet to search for images of Micro Pigs–type the link below to perform this search in Google:

http://goo.gl/JmB2og

You'll find that the most common results returned are of the piglets and not usually of the adults.

Occasionally newspapers or magazines will write a story about these pigs and the same problem occurs. You'll see pictures of the piglets and none of the adult pigs.

Why does this happen and what is the reason behind it? Simple; the piglets look cute and cute piglets make the articles more enjoyable. Typically you'll see a cute little piggy in a teacup, or pictured with some celebrity, yet you'll never usually see images of the fully grown adults (unless it's some horror story of tiny pig turning into a 700lb giant farm hog). If the article does contain information about the adults, it's often relegated to a few lines at the bottom of page.

When we were breeding Micro Pigs we provided as much information as possible. We were one of the first UK breeders to display a size chart on our website (see opposite page). We include plenty of photos of our adults on our website as well.

We also allowed any serious buyers to come and visit our farm to see our pigs in person. Quite a few of the visitors to our farm were shocked by size of them.

We believe that seeing the pigs is the best way to dispel the myths surrounding the breed. Also, it's the best way to show people what's involved when taking care of a Micro Pig.

We had plenty of visitors to our farm who left disappointed, but happy. I think we prevented a lot of people from buying a pet they neither had the correct environment, nor home in which to take sufficient care of one.

My point is this: any good breeder should allow you to come and see their pigs in person – in fact, a good breeder should encourage you to come and view them. They should also be knowledgeable about the breed and its requirements. If they aren't, take your business elsewhere–don't take the risk. If they're clueless about the piglets they're selling, they were probably clueless when they bought their parents.

If you've been looking at classified adverts (either online or in magazines) for Micro Pigs, you'll probably see the same claims being made by the sellers. They will usually be declaring that they have the smallest pigs in the business, and their pigs are inches smaller than the next seller's. Usually they'll have a few blurry photos, taken from the best angle possible, to back up their erroneous claims. Some breeders in the adverts might be telling the truth, other will be bending it, and others will be outright lying!

(cm)

Adult Micro pig
(3 years old)
50 cm

Adult Labrador
57cm

Average height
of a human male
176,8 cm

Adult Gloucester Old Spot pig
(boar)
75 cm

Personally I find this pitch flawed. Why? The reason is simple, and it's something that we used to tell every customer who visited our farm.

'The way you treat an animal makes a far bigger difference to its behaviour than whether the animal is large or small. The size of the pig (to a degree) does not make it easier or harder to keep. A pig which has been spoilt, or treated badly, will be a pain in the backside to keep regardless of whether it's big or small. A couple of inches aren't going to make things any easier.'

Any pig which has been treated properly, kept outdoors correctly, and has not been spoilt, can be a real pleasure to keep.

Pig Scams and Bad Breeders

All piglets, regardless of the breed, are small when they are born. A Micro Pig is only a few inches tall when born; piglets like the large white, and other hogs, are also a similar size when born. Even after a few weeks you'd only see a few inches difference in height between the two breeds if you could compare them side by side. It would take a few months for the size difference between the breeds to become apparent.

This makes the mis-selling of piglets easy. During the first few weeks of their lives it's easy to pass other breeds off as a miniature pig. Sometimes this is done intentionally, and by the time the unwitting pig owner knows something's wrong, the rogue breeder is gone. The pig usually ends up becoming far bigger than was promised, and the unlucky owner usually hasn't the means to take care of the hog properly.

Another scam is where a buyer has bought a pig from a clueless breeder. This breeder is ignorant of the animals he himself has bought–but has decided to breed and sell them anyway. The piglets either ends up the size of a farm hog, or they're a completely unsuitable breed for the buyer's home–they've been sold a pig prone to rooting or an aggressive breed.

Other clueless breeder antics involve selling pigs and providing no advice on how to keep them as a pet correctly. They inform the new owners that it's fine to feed a pig cat food (as they're omnivores) or that it's fine to feed the pig on weaner feed for the rest of its life – neither of which are true. These are just a couple of examples of the bad practice I've heard of over the years. These clueless breeders are not malicious, they're just idiots.

A pig is fully grown by around 3-5 years old. However, a pig can breed when it's as young as one year old. Some bad breeders will then sell the piglets, from a year old pig, and claim they'll only grow to the size of their mother. The buyers don't realise that the mother pig still has some growing to do herself, meaning the piglets will be bigger than the promised size. Although pigs between 1-3 years old don't grow much in height they do fill out, especially around their waste and rump.

One of the worst scams I've seen is where the breeder starves the piglets to keep their size down. They also usually finish the weaning early to aid this process. Not only is this downright cruel, it significantly increases the chances of health and mental problems in the pigs as they get older (more about his later). Healthy piglets should not have their bones showing through their skin–they should be energetic, bright and alert.

It's Going to Stay Small

Another situation I've seen and read about in the news, where a buyer has bought a legitimate Micro Pig, but it has then grown beyond what the buyer expected. The buyer is unhappy as he thought his pig would be much smaller than its parents.

All I can say is simply this–do not let your heart rule your head. If you have bought a Micro Pig and you have seen its parents then you should have an idea of what you are going to be dealing with once the pig reaches adulthood.

Viewing the parents will only give you a rough idea of size. The pig you could buy could be slighter bigger or smaller than its parents, there is nothing you can do about it, this is nature at work. Good Micro Pig breeding lines should, on average, produce young which are slightly smaller than the parents—even then you'll be looking at a few centimeters at the most.

However, if you have been sold a pig and the breeder has claimed that the pig should grow to be substantially smaller the sizes I've mentioned previously, this is a different area of concern. You should be very dubious about claims where the breeder states that their animals are well below 14"-26" height average. To my knowledge there are no breeds worldwide which are significantly smaller than those heights. Steer clear of anyone promising claims like this as they'll probably be bogus.

Conclusion about Micro Pig Size

This chapter highlights the importance of finding a good breeder, one who knows the breed and provides you with good quality information and advice. It can be difficult to find a good Micro Pig breeder as there are no registered micro clubs monitoring the breed or its breeders.

A few key steps to take are:

• Ask the breeder plenty of questions—do they appear knowledgeable? Do the answers they provide tie in with the things you've read in this and other books?

• Ask for testimonials—some breeders might be able to provide written testimonials or put you in contact with previous customers.

• Look for a breeder who's been established for a few years. If they have had a website online for a few years that's a start. If they were a 'fly-by-night' breeder chances are they probably won't have gone to the trouble of maintaining a website.

• Ask on Internet forums—in the useful links section at the end of this book there are links to websites where you can ask questions. Also there are many animal forums and Q&A sites you can ask your questions on. These could help.

The key to this process is—do your research before committing to anything and don't rush in. The best way to stop yourself from being scammed is to arm yourself with knowledge. Most bad breeders, in my experience, don't know a lot about pigs. Make sure you do.

Here are a few extra points worth considering:

• If you want the very smallest pigs possible buy black piglets. They have more Potbellied genes in them, this results in black micro pigs being smaller, on average, than their coloured counterparts. Usually they are cheaper as well. Good quality Potbellied Pigs can be very small—so they are worth considering.

• Coloured Micro Pigs are usually bigger than the black pigs. They have the DNA of other pig breeds in them. This results in their size, shape and frame being bigger than that of black piglets.

• As stated earlier, and from our own experience of breeding these pigs, the size and shape of the animal does not make them easier or harder to keep. The most important aspect of keeping a pet pig is how it is treated and making sure it is provided with the correct home environment.

• Pigs are fully grown when they are around three years old. When you are looking at piggy parents make sure you find out how old they are. If the piglets' parents are under three years of age, they themselves will grow a little more—the piglets you are viewing will potentially grow to be bigger than their parents.

Chapter 3 - Buy a Pig or Adoption

As discussed in the previous chapter, there's no defined standard of Micro Pig. The shape and size of the animal can vary, depending on whether or not it's a coloured Micro Pig or black one. However, both type of pig share similar characteristics and these are things we need to look out for when choosing stock.

It's worth noting that many of the points below can be used when buying a Kune Kune or a Potbellied Pig.

When it comes to owning a pet pig I would urge people to try the sanctuaries first before thinking of buying one. The sanctuaries take in thousands of pigs every year and many of them never get rehomed. Not only can you save some money, you'll be doing a great thing and helping an animal who needs a home. Also some sanctuaries are very experienced with pet pigs so you'll be getting a pig from an expert. For a list of sanctuaries see the end of this book.

Points to Consider

Every pig is an individual. Some are noisy, others are quiet. Some are timid, others love attention. Some can be aggressive, others are tame. Observe and examine the pig thoroughly and make sure they're suitable for your home.

Make sure you take the following points into consideration when viewing stock:

• The golden rule when buying a pet pig is this; make sure you see the adults of any piglet you intend to buy. You need to see the piggy parents in person. Ideally, you want to see the sow with her young.

• The boar of the piglets will usually be kept separate from the mother till around the ten week mark. If the piglets you are viewing are under ten weeks old, and they are being kept separate from the rest of the herd, ask to see the breeding boar which has been used to father the piglets.

• You will often find that bad breeders will be unwilling to let you see the piglets with their mother or father. When you see the parents you need to ask yourself: do I have the correct environment and enough room to take care of a pig this size?

• Please note, photographs of the parent pigs are not evidence alone. Photos can be faked, doctored, and misused. We've seen photos from our website turn up on dodgy sites and in classified advertisements. This illustrates that photographs of the animal you intend to buy cannot be trusted 100%–it also highlights again the importance of seeing any pigs in person.

• Some pigs can be noisy. If you have neighbours make sure you ask them before committing to anything. You don't want a noisy pig creating problems for you and them.

Adopting from a Sanctuary

Sanctuaries are a great option for anyone wanting a pet pig. If you choose to adopt, rather than buy, you could save yourself a lot of money. Also, you'll be helping an animal which really needs a home–possibly one that's been abandoned or has had a tough time.

Thousands of pigs are abandoned every year, and sanctuaries usually struggle to find enough homes to rehouse these pigs. Some of them will never be rehomed due to health or behavioral problems. However, this doesn't stop the sanctuaries taking care of these animals and providing them with a good home.

So, why not help the sanctuaries out and save yourself a bit of cash? Adopting a pig from a sanctuary has many advantages, some of them are:

• Most sanctuaries know their animals well; they'll be able to fit the personality of the pig to the owner.

• Some sanctuaries are experts in swine care; they'll be able to show you how to take care of the animal properly.

• Most sanctuaries verify new owners before allowing them to take home an animal. This ensures that owner is capable (and has the means) to take care of the pig properly.

• Some of the big sanctuaries routinely castrate and spay all their pigs. This will save you a lot of money and will also make the pig significantly easier to keep.

The chances are you'll probably end up with an adult pig. This is because most pigs are abandoned due to them becoming too big for the owners and their homes. Adopting an adult pig has many advantages: firstly, the pig will be fully grown and secondly, the pig will have matured and passed adolescence. Taking care of a fully grown pig means there won't be any hidden surprises regarding size. Also, pigs that are slightly older can be more relaxed and easier to keep.

Pig Behavioural Problems

Pigs can have behavioural problems such as aggression, tendencies to bite, a wariness of humans, or other bad behaviour. A common cause of these problems is trauma and previous bad treatment in the past.

Rehoming a pig with behavioural problems is a very honourable thing to do, but make sure you can take care of the animal properly first. A pig like this might not be safe around small children; it might also need plenty of space and extra room.

Pig sanctuaries save lots of pigs like this from bad owners. The good thing is that a pig sanctuary will fit the personality of the pig to the owner. They won't let you take a pig with problems home unless they are sure you can look after it properly.

Being Offered a Pig

Sometimes people are offered a pig for free. Again, this is not a decision to be taken lightly. Over the years I've been contacted by various people who've been in this position. They've been given a pig only to have unexpected problems (and vet bills) later down the line. You need to make sure you ask the right questions before you take on this responsibility.

Below are just a few of the questions you need to answer before committing to anything:

• Do I have enough room for this pig?

• How big will this pig grow and how old is it (bear in mind that pigs are not fully grown until 3-5 years of age)?

• Is the pig part of a pair or more? Do I have room for more than one animal?

• Is the pig healthy?

• Does the pig look fat or underweight?

• Does the pig have any behavioral problems? Will it be safe around my family?

• What's the pig's medical history? Is there one?

• What breed is the pig?

• Is the pig noisy? Will my neighbors be happy about the noise?

• Is the pig being fed the correct diet?

• Where is the pig being kept now?

• What conditions is it being kept in?

- Is the pig intact? (un-castrated/un-spayed)?

- If the pig is female, is she pregnant? (You need to be 100% sure of this).

- How old is the pig?

- Does the owner have an honest reason for giving the pig away?

- Do I have the finances to take on the pig, especially if it needs regular treatments by a vet?

There's nothing wrong with taking on a free animal–you might be doing someone a favour whilst saving a bit of cash. But don't rush in; make sure you do your homework, and examine every animal thoroughly.

A good vet who's knowledgeable about pigs can really help in these situations. The vet may cost, but they'll be able to spot problems you can't. It could save you a lot of stress, and money, in the future if they happen to find something serious before you take on an unknown pig.

Use the information in the rest of this book to answer the above questions before committing to anything. Make sure you are as well prepared as possible.

Taking on a pig (or pigs) in need of a new home is a good thing – however, the above points just go to show that it's not a decision to be rushed.

Finding a Good Breeder

Just as in life, there are good and bad people in the pig breeding industry. But how do you sort the good breeders from the bad ones. This chapter covers the things you need to look out for when choosing a breeder.

Finding a breeder who's been established for a few years is a great first step. The longer they've kept pigs the better. If they have been breeding for a few years they might have previous customers who could testify how good their pigs are.

The best way to find a good breeder is to do your research: ask around, look on the Internet, or ask someone who already owns a pet pig if they can recommend anyone. Or even ask a vet.

A good breeder should encourage viewings of their herd, not just the parents. You should always view a pig's parents; this will help you to gauge the adult size of your future pet. It'll also allow you to interact with parents and you'll be better able to judge their temperament.

A good breeder will be happy to answer any questions you have. They should be knowledgeable about the breed they keep and have confidence in what they do. Make sure you ask plenty of questions. Breeders who shy away from your questions, or provide bad or vague answers, should be avoided.

A good breeder will work with a veterinarian. Any decent breeder will need a veterinarian to maintain the health and welfare of their herd. Vets are needed to perform many tasks on pet pigs, including: castration, spaying, administration of drugs, check-ups, and diagnoses. Ask the breeder about their vet and how he helps?

When viewing pigs make sure you pay close attention to the condition of the animals; does any of the herd look sick, injured, lethargic, lame or thin? Where are the pigs kept and does this area look clean? Are the pigs well kept? Do they have a good temperament? These are just a few of the questions you need to ask yourself.

When looking at piglets you need to take the whole litter into consideration, not just the ones that you like. Observe the condition of the piglets as a whole. Do all the piglets look healthy and full of energy? Do they look clean and well fed? Are the piglets properly socialised? Find out when weaning will be finished?

A good breeder should provide after sales support. You should be able to call them in times of crisis, and they should be there to advise should problems arise. If this is your first pig then this level of support is invaluable.

A good breeder should provide some (or all) of the following: care guides, feeding instructions, size guarantees and a vaccination schedule. If you're buying a Kune Kune or Potbellied pig, your breeder might be able to provide you with a genetic history and pedigree record.

A good breeder should ask you as many questions as you ask them–they'll want their pigs to go to a suitable home. They should be asking questions about your set-up and how you're planning to keep your pigs. Be concerned if the breeder doesn't take an interest in you or they don't ask you much?

Here a few questions we used to ask our customers:

- Have you seen these type of pigs before?

- Are you aware of how big they grow?

- Where are you planning to keep your pig?

- How much room will the animal have?

- How are you planning to stop your pet from becoming bored?

- What are you planning to feed your pet?

- Have you visited other breeders? If so, what have they told you about the breed?

The above are just an example of some of the questions a decent breeder will ask you.

Too Good To Be True?

Just remember that if a deal sounds too good to be true, it probably isn't true. Good quality pigs cost money. When you take into account feeding, housing, vet bills, stud fees, advertising, etc., the costs quickly mount up. Quality animals are more expensive to buy, as you are paying for the time and care that has gone into the breed–pigs are no different. If you see offers for pigs that are ridiculously cheap then you should be suspicious. If the seller is claiming that their bargain piglets will end up being the size of cat, or something similar, you should be really suspicious.

If you like a particular breeder and they have no piglets for sale, ask them if they have a waiting list. Sometimes it's worth waiting for good stock to become available, rather than rushing and buying the first pigs you come across.

Make sure you buy the best quality pig you can afford. Your pig may live to be anything up to twenty years old, so try to buy the best genes and healthiest pig possible. You may regret the decision later it if you don't.

When dealing with Micro Pigs it might be worth paying a veterinarian, or asking an experienced pig keeper, to take a look at the piglets you intend to buy. This might cost, but, it may prevent from you from buying counterfeit pigs. Unless you're experienced with pigs it can be hard to determine whether the piglets you're looking at are genuine Micro Pigs or not. Get an expert to view them if you have any doubts.

Be careful when buy from classified ads or notice boards. These are the favourite haunts of the bad and rogue breeders. These breeders set up shop overnight, sell their bad pigs, and then disappear. When things go wrong for the unlucky owner, or the piglets grow into huge pigs, these bad breeders are often nowhere to be seen.

Be careful if a breeder is only willing to drop a piglet off at your property or home, and not let you view the piglet at their farm or premises. If a breeder makes an offer like this, and they're unwilling to let you see their herd or the parent pigs, then take your business elsewhere. This seems to be a common way people are scammed into buying a counterfeit pig.

Chapter 4 - Pig Age & Physical Features of Pigs

Calculating a Pigs Age

How can you find out how old a pig is? Well, this isn't easy, but with the help of a vet, or a pig expert, it is possible to make an educated guess.

A good breeder will keep a record of when their pigs are born. However, it's not uncommon for bad breeders to lie about the age of their pigs, thus making their pigs seem small for their age. Again, this highlights the importance getting a pig from a reputable breeder or a sanctuary.

Height and Size

Pigs are fully grown around 2-3 years of age, but, they may have an occasional growing spurt between the ages of 3-5 years. A vet, or a pig expert, could assess your pig's size and give you their opinion on its age.

Teeth & Tusks

Pigs' teeth can also be used as a way of estimating their age. Most pigs have two sets of baby teeth, and a final set of adult teeth after they're two years old. A vet, or a pig expert, should be able to view a pigs teeth and make an estimate how old the pig is.

Tusks can be used to guess the age of males. Usually boars will grow protruding tusks at around 2-3 years of age. The eye teeth (which grow into tusks in males) grow throughout a pig's whole life. Females can get 'tuskettes' later in their lives. A sow with these will probably be around 10 years old or more.

Weight

Weight can be used as a rough guide but there are drawbacks. On average, a pet pig should gain a pound a week from birth, so a year-old pig will be roughly 52lb in weight. However this method will only work if the pig has put weight on in a healthy manner, they must not be overweight. This method is useless with fat pigs. Also, different breeds may gain weight more quickly than others. This method can only be used as a very rough guide at best.

Behaviour

Behaviour can also indicate a pig's general age. Piglets grow fairly quickly until they're roughly two years old. Once a piglet reaches two you may notice a change in their behaviour, at two years old, your pig has become an adult. This is the age where they'll try to assert their dominance over the rest of the herd (this includes you and your family). They may start to fight more, become aggressive and naughty. This is perfectly natural behaviour for a pig but can be problematic for the owner. Pig training can help to minimise the problems that may arise when the pig reaches the terrible twos (we'll cover more on this subject later).

Once a pig is four years old their behaviour should have mellowed. Pigs older than four are usually very chilled out and relaxed (excluding pigs with behavioural problems).

A pig's behaviour can only be used as a very rough guide to determine their age.

Female Pig's Behaviour

Females start coming into heat at around 6 months of age. Signs include a swollen vulva, a change in mood or behaviour, and they may become noisier(they will whine and moan).

If you stand behind her and place your hand on her back, and she doesn't move then she's probably in heat. If you've adopted an older female that doesn't come into heat, she's probably been spayed.

Pig Age Conclusion

As this section shows, there is no real way to determine a pig's age accurately. Pig's teeth are the best method, but even this will only give you an approximate age. If you're unsure, get an experienced pig owner or a vet to take a look at the animal. They will be able to make a better guess than you.

Physical Features of Healthy Pigs

Learning what constitutes a healthy pig is essential. Not only will it help you when buying stock, it'll also help you if you ever need to diagnose pet if they are ever ill.

Head

Ears—should be clean and warm. They should be erect and not floppy. The ears should not lop over the eyes.

Eyes—Eyes can vary in colour; they should be clear looking. The pig's eyes should be alert and responsive.

Nose—A pig should not have a runny nose. Its nose should be cold to touch and slightly moist. The pig should also be able to breathe through it easily.

Feet—The pig should look level and not be limping. Make sure you watch the pig when moving, ensure that it moves evenly and without a limp or discomfort. The pig should distribute its weight evenly on all feet. Each foot should have two toes which should be neat and tidy, and equal in length. Adult pigs' toes can become overgrown so keep an eye out for toes which appear long in length, uneven, or that bend upwards.

If you are buying or adopting an adult pig and the animal appears to have overgrown toes you will need to trim them. Excessive toe length can stretch the tendons of the hoof and leaving it untreated can cripple a pig in later life.

Body, Tails, Rump

Body—should be even looking and symmetrical. Ribs can be seen slightly, on some pigs, but the pig shouldn't be excessively thin. Thin pigs might mean the breeder is under feeding them, or it could be a sign that the animal is ill.

Piglets—should look chubby and well rounded. Piglets younger than five weeks old have a large head in proportion to their bodies.

Adult—a pig's body shape varies depending on sex. Sows tend to have a more rounded shape; boars tend to be leaner looking, thinner and longer in length.

Tails—Micro Pigs and Potbellies should have straight tails, they shouldn't be curly. A curly tail could indicate another breed. Kune Kunes' tails can be curly, but these pigs are easily recognisable due to their unique hair style and colours (see the Kune Kune section earlier in the book for more details).Also, a pig's tail should never be wet or dirty. Backsides and bums should be clean and not soiled. A dirty bottom could be a sign that the pig is sick or ill.

Hair and Skin

These should be healthy looking and shiny. The condition of the pig's hair can vary depending on the time of year. A pig's coat can become dull looking during winter.

Very young piglets' hair can be soft to touch; an adult's coat is usually bristly and can be thin looking with age.

Most pigs can have a winter and summer coat of hair. Usually they shed their coat around autumn; this is called 'blowing the coat'. When they're in between coats, they may have bald patches and suffer from hair loss, this is perfectly normal.

You should be concerned if a pig has uneven bald patches, and red and inflamed skin. This could indicate that the pig has mites or some other illness.

Poo/Faeces

Poo and excrement can be a good indicator of the health of a piglet. Their poo should be fairly hard and solid. Be wary if the excrement is very soft, runny or has traces of blood in it. These can be signs that the pig you are viewing is sick.

Pigs are very clean animals. They do not poo in their beds. Usually they find an area or spot to poo in, and they continue to use it. If there are sizeable amounts of poo in their bed then this could be an indicator that something's wrong.

Size and Weight

The rule of thumb concerning piglets and healthy weight gain is this—a piglet should gain approximately one pound of weight per week. So, a year-old pig should weigh approximately 52lbs. However, you can only use this technique for a piglet which has been fed correctly. If they've been overfed or underfed this way of measuring their age won't work.

Does the pig look thin or fat? A thin pig isn't usually a problem, they may have been underfed or have an infestation of worms. Other causes can sometimes be an internal blockage or constipation. Canned pumpkin can be used to help a constipated pig's bowel movements. More severe blockages may need to be diagnosed by a vet using x-ray.

An overweight pig can suffer all manner of health problems, such as: becoming lame, a higher risk of becoming blind and a higher risk of arthritis. An obese animal may need to be placed on a diet to help him/her lose weight. It can be a tough job to slim a pig—they are very stubborn animals, changing their diet can lead to them becoming noisy, aggressive and problematic.

Just like us, when a pig reaches its senior years (around ten years or older) it's more prone to the afflictions of old age. Arthritis is a big problem for senior pigs; there's always a chance that you will have to purchase medication to relieve the worst of their symptoms. We'll be covering senior pigs in more detail later in this book. The best way to identify possible health problems is to get a vet to take a look at the pig before you commit to anything.

Personality

Piglets should be non-aggressive and docile. Young piglets are naturally curious about new objects, people and experiences. They'll approach new things, sniff them, nibble at them and even bite them (be careful of their sharp teeth). Young piglets should be full of energy and vitality. They should be happily running and darting about their pen/field and they should be noisy – they will sometimes growl and bark. Be wary of sickly looking piglets that appear weak and lethargic – this could be an indicator that something's wrong.

Adult pigs should also be non-aggressive and docile. They might be wary of new faces and visitors so don't be worried if the adult you are looking at keeps a short distance away from you. This can be worked on over time.

Pigs respond well to tone of voice and commands, so try talking to them when you get up close. Observe which ones seem the most responsive and friendly. Don't just choose a pig, let them choose you.

Conclusion

When viewing stock you need to be able to walk away if you think the pigs are not up to standard. Do not let your heart rule your head. You need to buy the healthiest stock with the best genes you can afford. Buying anything less, or purchasing a sickly animal, could lead to additional vet bills and heartache in the future.

Also, make sure you look at as many different breeders and stock as possible. This will help you build up a better picture of what makes good and bad stock.

A pig can live to around twenty years old, so you need to make sure you get everything right at the beginning to ensure you, and your new pet's, happiness. Just remember, 100% health cannot be guaranteed, but if you follow all our guidelines you'll be off to a good start.

Chapter 5 - Which Sex is Best?

Males (Boars, Barrows)

Unless you are planning to breed from them, boars need to be castrated. Don't buy an intact male as a pet, they're controlled by their hormones and are therefore, untrainable. Just like an un-castrated dog, an intact boar will attempt to mate with everything in sight once they reach adolescence. They're often very badly behaved, noisy, and smelly and can be quite destructive.

Castrated males (Barrows) are far easier to keep as pets. Compared with a sow, they seem to have a more laid back attitude. Once they have passed through adolescence, a barrow will usually become lazier as they get older. They tend to sleep more than females as well, making them easier to keep.

Barrows tend to be bossed about by sows of a similar size and height—especially if the females are un-spayed. This will be more noticeable around feeding times or when the pigs are trying to get your attention.

Females (Sows)

Un-spayed (intact) sows will first come into season (hogging) at around three months old. They'll then come into season roughly every three weeks, usually the hogging lasts around three days.

Hogging behaviour varies, depending on the individual. During this time they may appear grumpy, disobedient, noisy, and destructive. Unlike female dogs, pigs do not produce a bloody discharge.

With our own sows, we find that they all behave differently when in season. One particular sow shows no change in her behaviour at all, and the only way to tell she is in season is when the boar becomes interested in her, or when the other sows jump on her back. She makes no noise and never chews or destroys anything. Yet when our other sows come into season they become more vocal and noisy. One sow chews and bites a wooden gate leading into her pen; the other sow makes less noise but will follow you around like a sheep.

Pigs have sharp teeth and strong jaw muscles so can cause significant damage when chewing on things. You will need to make sure that their pen is robust enough to withstand such damage when they are in season.

During hogging your pig's training will go out of the window. A sow in season is ruled by her hormones and nothing else. It's very common for a pig in season to ignore their usual poo area and just urinate anywhere. This might be a problem if your pig is kept inside your house, but if you keep your pig outside this is less of an issue.

The experience we've had with our own pigs has shown us that it's really pot luck what sort of behaviour an intact sow will show when she's in season. Personally, we've found that as long as they are kept outdoors, behind good quality fencing, their seasonal temper tantrums and moods are easily dealt with.

But, make sure the potential noise and the destructiveness aren't a problem for you, your neighbors, or your home.

If all the above sounds like too much trouble then you may want to have your sow spayed. Spaying eliminates all their sexual behaviour and turns them into a great pet. To learn more about spaying see the next chapter.

Chapter 6 - Spaying and Castration

Spaying Your Pig

Female piglets will start coming into heat as early as three months of age, they become sexually active around 5-6 months of age. Spaying is usual performed on the sow after their second heat, ideally at around 5-8 months old. The operation itself is similar to the one performed on female dogs–the ovaries are removed. But, due to the anatomy of a pig, things are slightly more complex.

Once a sow is around eight months old they will start to put on excess fat. This makes the operation difficult as the vet will have to cut through this fat to get to the ovaries. If you want to spay a pig older than eight months old, consult your vet; you may need to slim the animal to make the operation safer to perform.

Spaying a pig will eliminate the monthly bad moods and any other hogging behaviour. A spayed female can be taught and it's also possible to potty train them. You can potty train an intact pig, but once their heat kicks in they will forget this training.

Another important effect of spaying is that it also reduces the risk of the pig developing cancers and uterine infections (Pyometria); these are diseases which can affect a sow later in its life.

You will need to find a vet who is familiar with performing the operation on pigs. Your local vet might not have the necessary experience. Try contacting a few different surgeries until you find someone who's familiar with performing the operation. It might be worth contacting your nearest veterinarian university if you cannot find a local vet with the necessary experience.

Checking if a Pig is Spayed or Pregnant

Over the years I've been contacted by several people who've been given pigs, only to find that they were pregnant. Their new pig has given birth, and the new owners have then to try and find new homes for the piglets. Raising piglets is not an easy task, especially for a novice pig keeper, it's even harder when it catches you unprepared.

If you are rehoming an intact female, make sure that she didn't have the chance to become fertilised. Has the sow had any contact with any intact boars? Male pigs can be fertile at 9 weeks; females become fertile around 6 months of age. If the sow is 5 months or older, un-spayed, and has been kept with any intact males, she may be pregnant.

How do you know if a pig is spayed? Well, it's very hard to tell if spaying has been performed. A vet is probably the only person who could tell with any degree of accuracy, and even then, they'd have to perform a thorough examination to be 100% sure.

The only way to accurately confirm pregnancy is, again, to let the vet make a thorough examination, possibly using ultrasound.

Early pregnancies are hard to spot unless you know the pig and its monthly heats. Late pregnancies are easier to spot due to the sow becoming huge. Also, during the last few weeks of their pregnancy you can sometimes touch the sow's belly and feel the piglets moving in the womb.

Unless you know the sow well, do not use their heats for pregnancy diagnosis, it's far too easy to make a mistake. Get a vet to take a look if you have any doubts.

If you are buying or adopting a sow which is five months, or older, and it has been kept in a mixed-sex herd, get it checked out. If you don't, you could end up with more pigs than you bargained for.

Chapter 7 - Getting Your Home Ready

I t's essential to have everything ready before you bring your new pet home. You do not want to be moving and changing things when your pigs are trying to settle in.

Outdoor Pigs

Personally, from our own experience, we believe that pigs should be kept outside in an adequate sized space. It makes their care a lot easier.

One pig should have access to at least thirty square feet of space, where they can play, graze, and move around. Two pigs ideally would need around sixty square feet of space.

A small, secondary pen should also be provided for your pet pig. Ideally this should surround their home or shed. The purpose of the smaller pen is to allow you to confine the pig when needed. A pen like this is handy if you need to get hold of your pet, when you need to separate them, or so you can place them inside it when they misbehave.

The optimum size for this smaller pen is around fifteen square feet. Good quality fencing should be used in the construction of any pig pen. Even a pet pig, especially when fully grown, has enough strength and power to break through weak or poor fencing.

The more space your pig has the better, as this will help prevent your pet from becoming bored. A bored pig is a problem pig.

Wallows and Shade

A wallow should also be provided during the summer and hot months. This is essential; it will allow your pet to cool off during hot days. Pigs do not sweat so they use a wallow as a way to cool down. A wallow can be a muddy pool of water, or a child's paddling pool with a few inches of water added.

If you do use a paddling pool as a wallow, don't fill it too deep, and make sure your pig can get in and out of it easily. Your pig will want to be able to lay down in it, so an inch or two of water should be sufficient. Some pigs hate paddling pools, others love them.

Alternatively you can make a more traditional muddy wallow. We usually dig a hole a few inches deep and a few feet wide. We place plastic sheeting in the hole and fill it back in with earth. We then add water to make the hole muddy. On hot days the pigs usually can't wait to get in and cool off.

Also, make sure that you provide some shade for your pig. They can suffer from heat stroke and sunburn if they cannot cool down or find a place out of direct sunlight.

Steep & Slippery Surfaces

Pigs are not the most sure-footed animals; they struggle on very steep surfaces or slippery ground. Be careful when the ground is slippery, icy or snow covered–your pig could easily slip and injure themselves.

Pigs naturally try to avoid slippery areas. Sometimes when conditions are slippery you might need to provide your pig with a path, so they can move about safely. You might need to remove any snow, place grit over ice, or cover slippery mud with bark chippings before they are happy moving around.

Slippery wooden panels, flooring and decking can also be a problem. A few old, rubber car mats will also help their grip on such surfaces.

Very steep surfaces should be physically altered or fenced off. Although a pig will naturally avoid surfaces like these, they can sometimes trip and fall down them. I've also known pigs to be knocked down steep hills when they've been fighting, so take this into consideration when planning your pig pen.

Toilet

A small part of their outdoor space will be used as a toilet. Although pigs themselves do not smell their poo does. You'll need to dispose of it as you see fit. Pig poo does make excellent compost though, so will come in handy for fertilising your plants. Alternatively you could always throw it in the bin. Flushing their poo down the toilet could be quite hard as their stools are long and hard – they may get jammed.

Pigs tend to pick a potty spot, and then stick to it. This makes cleaning up their mess very easy, when compared with other animals. We found it helpful to place a large, flat board down (where the pig has chosen its potty spot), after the pig goes to the toilet simply lift the board and throw the pig poo on the compost heap, or in the bin.

A pig can be potty trained, but you must be prepared to put the time in to achieve this.

More about this later in this book.

Grazing

Ideally, part of their space should contain grass so they can graze. Grass provides them with extra nutrition; it also gives their mouth something to do, and prevents them becoming bored. If your pig does not have access to any grass, try to provide them with a bit of hay, haylage or silage for them to munch on: make sure it isn't mouldy as it could make them ill.

Rooting

Rooting is a perfectly natural behaviour and has to be accepted. In the wild they use this behaviour to find food, like acorns and truffles. A ring placed in the nose is the usual solution to unwanted rooting, but this can cause the pig pain and discomfort.

Whether your pig will root depends on a lot of factors. Potbellies and Kune Kune are less prone to rooting due to their small snouts.

Some Micro Pigs are more prone to rooting than others, as the shape of their heads can vary. The rule of thumb is this—the longer the snout the greater the tendency to root.

But the type of ground the pig is kept on plays a role as well. If the ground is very hard then the pigs will root less, if it's soft you'll find they will root more.

Only you can decide whether or not the rooting is acceptable. If this behaviour is unacceptable you may have to isolate your pet to a particular spot to minimise the damage. We'll cover some possible solutions to minimise rooting later in this book.

A word of warning, pigs and landscaped gardens are usually a bad mix.

Sleeping Areas

A pig needs a place to sleep. This area needs to be dry and a place they can escape from bad weather. Also, the sleeping area needs to be cool during warm days and provide shade during hot weather.

A sleeping area can take many forms—it can be a shed, sty, stable, garage, etc.—as long it keeps the bad weather out, and provides shade when it's hot, it will be sufficient.

If you need to buy a pig home, get (or build) a standard garden shed. A 6ft x4ft shed is plenty big enough for a pair of pigs, and with a few easy modifications it can be a perfect pig home.

I find sheds to be better suited for pet pigs than your average pig sty/igloo. Sheds are easier to clean than sties as you can stand up in them, making them easier to clean out.

Usually you have to bend over to get inside a pig sty/igloo, this makes cleaning them a back-breaking chore. Also a shed with a door can be shut at night which is great for when the weather's really bad.

When using a shed for a pig house I'd recommend blocking out any windows. This will help reduce the temperature, inside the shed, during the summer months. Shed windows can act like a greenhouse during sunny days, they can also help lose heat during the winter months. Personally, I like to remove, or cover the windows up if possible.

Your local weather and climate will determine the properties your pig shed should have. If you suffer from very cold and severe winters you may need to insulate the sides and roof. If you do insulate your pig's home make sure you keep an eye on the temperature during the summer months, the extra insulation could make it too warm for your pet during the hotter months.

I also find that splitting the door into two is a good idea. This creates something which resembles a stable door, with a top and a bottom half. Doing this will allow you to shut the top during bad weather which will help keep your pet warm, and their straw dry. The door can be fully open during the hot months for added ventilation.

Sometimes fitting flaps to a door is a great way to help keep bad weather out. Rubber car mats are great for this job, and they're cheap.

When building your pig shed try to take into account the average direction of the wind in your area and home. Placing the shed's entrance downwind will help to keep their home warm and dry.

Provide your pig with plenty of barley for bedding. They love to immerse themselves in it and make a nest. This is how your piggy keeps warm. Barley straw is preferred over wheat straw as it tends to last longer and doesn't break down into dust as quickly. Give them plenty of extra straw in winter as this will help them keep warm.

Feeding Area

A feeding area and provisions should also be provided. A dog dish or a small trough should suffice. Feeding pigs from a trough or bowl means they waste less food.

During the wetter parts of the year you may want to try and feed your pigs on hard or well-drained ground (i.e. patio, concrete floor, etc.). Daily feeding in the same area, on soft wet ground, will result in the ground becoming muddy and messy.

Plants Bad for Pigs

The following plants are poisonous to pigs: -

- Foxglove

- Rhododendron

- Hemlock

- Laburnum

- Yew

- St. John's Wort

Usually pigs have a natural instinct to avoid eating things which are harmful to them.

As far as I'm aware they do have to eat a rather large quantity of the above before it has a bad effect on them. However, if you have any of the above plants in your garden, it might be worth keeping your pig away from them (fencing them off) or removing them altogether.

Chapter 8 - Pig Fencing

All pigs, once fully grown, have a lot of strength. Any fencing you place around them needs to be strong enough to prevent them from escaping, and strong enough to withstand any attempt at damage made by your pig. Your fencing also needs to be free of holes big enough for them to squeeze through–especially if you have small piglets. Also, your fencing has to be robust enough to keep other livestock out as well as potential predators–like dogs and coyotes.

Pigs have more of a tendency to go through or under fencing, rather than going over it; they'll use their fleshy nose to pry under things. Make sure that the bottom of any fencing is against the ground and not a couple of inches above it. A pig will also pull and swing on fencing, so you need to make sure that it can resist this type of damage.

Pigs have very sharp teeth and strong jaw muscles. They'll sometimes try to chew through fencing; selecting wood or wire gauge fencing, thick enough to withstand this damage, is essential. In-heat females are very prone to chewing and pulling on fencing, keep an eye on where they are causing the damage and repair immediately if needed.

Pigs do not burrow or dig, but they can wear away the ground by constantly walking on it. Keep a watchful eye on any fencing situated on soft ground; the surrounding area can wear down over time, eventually creating an escape hole for your pet.

Wire Fencing

Cattle/sheep fencing is a great way to contain your pigs and it's very cost effective. By using a dozen or more fence posts and a few rolls of wire, you can easily construct a massive pig paddock, if you have the room and time. This type of fencing is more suited to flatter ground but you can fit it to bumpy ground using a few extra posts and a little patience.

Choose a gauge of wire (strands) no less than 2.5mm to 3mm thick. Other types of fencing can be used, such as woven, or a stiffer type, but these are usually more expensive than cattle and sheep fencing.

Chicken wire (poultry mesh), on its own, is unsuitable to keep your pigs contained. Poultry fencing is not strong enough to resist the pigs when they start biting and pulling on it (and believe me, they'll try). It should be used in conjunction with cattle/sheep fencing; you can attach it to the cattle fencing via metal rings, or using a hog tying tool, to fill in the holes that small piglets might be able to squeeze through. However, pigs tend to bite and pull on any fencing, and chicken wire is prone to ripping; make sure you regularly check it and make repairs if needed.

Use 5ft wooden fence posts with your wire fencing, knock them roughly a foot into the ground. The posts need to be a minimum of three inches in diameter. I find that five inch diameter fence posts are best, they are sturdier and they should last for few years before needing to be replaced. You can use square or half round posts instead, as long as they are sturdy and a few inches thick, they should be okay.

Your fence posts should be situated approximately 4-6 yards apart. Additional fence posts might be needed if you're building on bumpy or hilly ground–add them in dips and hollows to help pull the fence down.

The corners of your pig pen will take the most stress; they'll be pulled inwards by the tightness of your wire fencing. You'll need to provide your corner posts with extra support, if you don't your fence will sag and it'll become loose over time. Reinforce the corner posts with diagonal struts, stuck in the ground at approximately 30– 45° angle; fix these into the ground and then connect to the corner post (see Figure 1).

When building your fence, make sure the wire fencing is pulled as tight as you can get it. If your fencing is loose your pigs might be able to escape underneath. Also it's better to run the fencing against the floor, rather than a few inches off the ground. Pigs tend to go under fencing, not over it. They'll use their noses, and their strong neck muscles, to shove themselves under any loose bits. The smaller you can make the gaps underneath your fencing the better.

Escape hole in a fence - The pig bent the fence up and forced its way underneath. The problem is made worse due to soft, wet ground surrounding the fence. In this case we added an additional fence post in the middle and fixed the wire mesh to it

Figure 1 - End section of a wire fence reinforced with diagonal post dug into the ground - Metal livestock fencing is great for adult pigs, just make sure your piglets can't squeeze through it though

If you're building a fence where other livestock is kept – such as: horses, cows, and sheep you may want to run a single strand of barbed wire along the top of the fence posts. This will help prevent livestock jumping over the fence; it'll also keep predators out (such as wild dogs and coyotes). It also stops horses and cattle from scratching themselves on the fence and damaging it.

Wooden Fencing

If you are housing your pigs in a backyard, allotment, or something similar, you may want to consider using wooden fencing as an alternative. Your pigs will chew, gnaw and pull on your fencing, so make sure you use fencing panels strong enough to resist damage. Also, make sure the wood has been treated with a wood preservative or else it may rot.

I find that 10-foot lengths of 3" x 1" wooden rails are suitable and cost effective for use in a wooden pig fencing setup. Use these with either 3-5" diameter fence posts (I prefer to use 5" posts due them being more durable). Four rails should be used per fence post section; the height of the top rail needs only to be two feet from the bottom. As stated previously, pigs tend to go under fencing, not over it, so a fence around four feet high will should suffice.

Just like the wire fencing, if you are building your fence in a field with other livestock around, consider running a strand of barbed wire on top of the fence posts. This will prevent damage, caused by other livestock scratching themselves against it, and it'll help keep predators out.

The great thing about wooden fencing is that it can be cut and contoured to suit the shape of your property. It's also pretty easy to create a nice tight fence which can take a lot punishment. Done right, it can look nice, and can be painted to suit your taste. Just make sure you use a non-toxic paint which is safe for use around animals.

If housing small piglets behind a wooden fence you might want to staple a layer of chicken wire to it, to prevent them squeezing through any gaps. Chicken wire/mesh is fine to use if it is attached to a strong robust fence.

Electric Fencing,

Electric fencing can be a very effective way of keeping your pig confined to a particular area. It's also a really handy thing to have in times of emergency (i.e. to patch up holes where your pigs may have broken out, etc.).

Electric fencing can also be used to strip-graze pigs in large fields or areas. To strip-graze, you simply confine the pigs to a particular part of the pasture for a period of time (usually a few weeks). Once the ground is tired or overgrazed, you set the fence up elsewhere, you then move your pigs into this new area and they can graze the new pasture. Obviously this is more suited to pig owners who have more land and space.

Single-strand electric fencing is probably the most effective and cost efficient. Do not use electric netting or poultry netting, it's easy for a pig to get tangled in it.

Plastic stranded wire, or fencing tape, is the best to use. Do not use a pure metal wire; it can severely cut animals if they ever become tangled in it.

If you are planning to breed pigs then electric fencing is often essential. It's sometimes the only way to keep the boars and sows apart. They'll often wreck normal fencing in an attempt to get to each other, especially when the sows come into heat. Setting up a single strand of electric tape or wire around the perimeter of their paddocks will minimise the damage done by pigs of a breeding age.

Basic Kit

A basic electric fence kit consists of a wire or electric tape, fence posts or hooks, and a charging kit.

Electric fences require regular maintenance to ensure that they run efficiently. You will need to routinely examine the path of the electric fence to ensure that no grass, or debris, is touching it. If any grass or debris is touching the wire it will earth it, and reduce its efficiency.

Our Wooden Pig fencing - Wire mesh has been fitted to the front to prevent them from chewing the wood

Battery and energiser - this is connected to a single strand of wire a few inches off the ground (although you cannot see the electric fence wire in this picture)

The wire strand or tape should be held to the fence posts using rubber or plastic mounts (or posts). You cannot attach electric tape, or wire, directly to wooden fence posts as this will earth the circuit and reduce its efficiency.

An electric fence needs a charging kit, these usually come in two types–mains driven or battery-powered. Any mains driven chargers need to be protected from the weather. Mains driven units are far more suited to permanent electric fence setups. If you are setting a mains charging kit up, employ a professional to fit it (unless you know what you are doing). Setting up a mains plug outside can be very dangerous if done incorrectly–if in doubt employ a professional to do it.

Battery-powered charging units are more suited to people who are using semi-permanent or mobile fencing arrangements. If you're using a battery-powered charger, check the battery regularly to ensure it hasn't gone flat (testers can be bought for this task). You also need a way of charging your depleted batteries when needed. If you are fortunate enough to live in a sunny climate you could use a solar powered charging kit. These systems actually work on the battery whilst it's in use in the field.

Chapter 9 - Watering Your Piggy

I t's very important that a permanent source of water is provided at all times. Your pet pigs, like humans, can suffer from salt poisoning through lack of water.

There are various ways to provide water to your pet. A large water dish or bucket is an excellent way to water your pet. However, if you're more DIY inclined; you may want to try fitting an automatic watering system for them. The advantage of an auto water system is that (providing the system is working) they will never run out.

This chapter covers the various options open to you with regards to watering your pig.

Figure 1: bucket & car tyre water feeder

Simple Watering System

One of the simplest ways to water your pet is using a bucket, placed in an old car tyre, with a large stone in the bottom (figure 1). The bucket wants to be the flatter wider type. The stone and tyre will help prevent the pigs tipping the bucket over.

Even if you do fit an automatic watering system, I thoroughly recommend that you always keep one or two of these simple water feeders spare. They're handy to have in times of emergency. We use them when our automatic watering systems break, or if they freeze in the winter.

Automatic Watering System

Some folk might want to opt for an automated water system. Any system like this requires a bit of DIY and plumbing. Also, a pig watering system is setup differently to the systems used by other livestock.

The great thing about an automatic water system is that you won't need to fill up your pig's water bucket every day.

If you're keeping a few pigs, an automatic water feeder is a must. It's surprising how much water, even two pigs, can consume on a hot day. And keeping your piggies hydrated is very important due to the risk of salt poising and dehydration.

Figure 2: plastic bowl type water feeder

Plastic or Metal Water Feeders: which are best?

In our opinion, large metal water drinkers are best. They're more durable, hard wearing, and they can usually hold more water than their plastic drinker counterparts. Also, metal drinkers seem able to withstand more damage.

Water bowls like the one pictured left (figure 2) can be used with pigs; however, we found them to have their disadvantages. A water bowl has to be placed within a few of inches of the ground to allow the pigs to drink. When placed close to the floor, these drinkers accumulate dirt and debris quickly. This is especially so when the bowl is used near soft ground, or mud.

When these bowls become dirty they do not work correctly: gradually the dirt will build up and replace the water in the bowl. These types of drinkers will need to be cleaned regularly if they're to work properly.

Header and Non Header Tank Water Systems

Header and non-header tank water systems are two types of automatic watering system that can be used with any livestock. The only real difference is that one has a header tank and the other is fed directly from the water main. Both systems have advantages and disadvantages which we will discuss.

The picture below (figure 4) is a header tank that we use in our own setup.

Regulators or reducers (white pipe in Figure 2 and 4) need to be fitted before the inlet valve–this reduces the mains pressure before it enters the inlet valve. If you don't add this you can blow the pipes apart, causing a nasty leak.

An overflow pipe (small white pipe at the rear of tank in Figure 4) should be fitted to the header tank; this overflow pipe should then be fed to a drain or to a place where a large spillage will do no damage.

Figure 3: Metal box water feeder. Far more robust and suited for pigs

Ensure that the header tank you are using has a tap at the base, to allow you to empty the tank; this makes things easier when you have to clean the tank, especially if it's a big tank.

It's best to use a header tank which will not allow sunlight to enter it. Any header unit which allows sunlight in will accelerate algae growth inside it. This means more cleaning out and sanitisation of the water tank.

The header tanks are then connected to the pig's water feeder or water bowl. This pipe will not be subjected to the same pressures that the mains water pipe is under, so a light duty pipe (such as rubber) can be used.

Any water tank will require cleaning from time to time. It's a good idea to empty the tank every so often, remove any waste which is present, and then scrub and disinfect it. We usually do this once or twice a year. It's also important that you make sure any header tank is covered or sealed when in use. This prevents biological matter, such as dead insects/leaves/etc., from falling into the water. Over time, this build-up of biological matter can contaminate the water and cause potential health problems–in extreme cases.

Figure 4: Small header tank plumbed into the mains

Personally I like using this type of watering system as it's easy to add a dose of nutrients (i.e. apple cider vinegar) to the pig's water. Also, if for some reason the mains water gets cut, you still have a full tank of water with which to supply your pigs.

You can also use this type of system to collect rain water which may reduce your water bill.

Header-less Water System

Figure 2 (plastic bowl feeder) shows a slightly different water system. In this system there is no header tank; water is fed directly, from the mains, to the water feeder. It is critical that a water pressure reducer (white pipe) is used before the water feeder. If you don't fit a reducer you run the risk of blowing the inlet valve in your water feeder.

Figure 5: Large water butt converted into a header tank

As with the previous water system, it's essential that you fit a stop tap as close to the mains end as possible. This will allow you to switch off your watering system in case of an emergency. The stop tap ideally needs to be situated underground, or housed inside, to prevent it from freezing during winter.

The advantage of this system is that it is usually cleaner than a header tank system. Muck and debris will not build up due to the lack of a header tank. This system is also cheaper to build, as it can be built with just a little bit of piping, a water feeder, and a T-splitter (shown below in figure 6).

Water Pipes

Plastic piping is needed to transfer water around your system. We usually use 25mm plastic pipe as it's fairly cost effective. Also, this diameter of pipe is needed to cope with the water pressure from the water mains.

When splitting the mains water pipe, ensure that you fit the stop tap on your new pipe. This tap wants to be as close to the mains side as possible. The stop tap allows you to shut off the water to your watering system, when needed, or in times of emergency.

Your water pipes and taps may need to be insulated or covered depending on your climate. Burying the pipe underground may help to insulate it, this can also be a great way of stopping your pigs chewing on the pipe and causing damage.

With our own water system we usually just switch it off on the coldest days; this prevents any split pipes and damage. During this time we simply revert to using the bucket and tyre method.

When using water pipes inside a pig pen it's good practice to have the bare minimum amount of pipe exposed. Pigs will easily chew through plastic piping so make sure it's out of reach. You can bury it, raise it so it's out of reach, or use a metal pipe for any exposed bits.

Figure 6: A T-Splitter allows simple splitting of a mains water pipe

Chapter 10 - Feeding Your Pig

What do you feed a pet pig? What treats can I feed them and what foodstuffs should I avoid? These are the question any serious pig owner should ask.

This part of the book is going to cover these questions in depth. By the end of this chapter you'll have a clear idea of what you should, or shouldn't, feed your pig.

Basic Feeding

Most vets agree that a mixed diet is the best for pet pigs. This includes their daily feed, some leafy green vegetables, and pasture to graze on.

An adult pig (1.5-2 years of age) requires approximately 1kg of non-fattening sow nuts per day. Slightly bigger pigs may require a little more (up to 0.5kg per day extra).

During winter their daily ration may be increased due to the lack of grazing vegetation and grass available. Or you can supplement the lack of grass with quality hay, fresh straw, silage or haylage.

If you are feeding your pig substantially more than the above amounts you risk the animal becoming fat. Obese pigs are more likely to develop health problems such as bad arthritis later in life. Fat pigs also usually have behavioural problems as they become food obsessed (more about this later).

Do not feed your pig any animal feeds which are designed for other animals. Animal feeds, such as the ones available for calves and sheep, may contain additives, antibiotics and minerals which may be bad for your pig. They may also be high in protein, also bad for your pig, and can cause them to become fat.

The only exception to this are certain types of horse feed. Horse feeds are often used in the large Potbellied Pig sanctuaries because they can be bought in 'bulk' quantities. Horse feeds are also handy if you live in a remote area and you're struggling to find a non- fattening pig feed; or dedicated Potbellied Pig feed.

When using horse feed you must use complete feed. Do not use sweet feed or your pig will become very fat, very quickly. Complete feed usually contains alfalfa, oats and rye wheat. Sweet feed usually contains molasses, sugar cane and corn syrups which are very tasty but also very fattening.

Pigs can easily develop a sweet tooth. Once this happens it can be very hard to switch them back to a feed with less fat and sugar.

Ideally, your pig should have two meals a day. Pig feed in the morning and some dark leafy greens in the afternoon. The second feed is especially important for pigs that cannot graze, as pigs can develop ulcers and an acid reflux through infrequent feeding (one meal a day). This risk is higher in piglets under six months old. Regular grazing, two meals a day and a constant supply of fresh water will help to prevent this happening.

Grazing

Pet pigs should be allowed to graze. They get a lot of roughage from eating grass. It's also a great way to prevent them becoming bored, and keeping their mouths busy also helps to keep them out of mischief.

If your pigs cannot graze provide them with some silage, haylage, hay or fresh straw. There's no specific amount of this type of forage you should feed your pet. The only real way you can tell whether or not your pig is eating too much of this type of food is to keep an eye on its weight. If your pig starts to look fat either cut down the amount of forage you're feeding them, or prevent them grazing.

Personally I find pigs prefer silage over hay. Just make sure that you feed your pigs good quality silage or haylage. This means it should be free from mould and growths. Mouldy silage can contain listeria which can be harmful to your pet.

Pig Feeds

There are different types of pig feed available, it's critical that you select the right one for your type of pig.

It's essential that you feed your pig **non-fattening** sow nuts—I cannot stress this enough. Ideally the pig feed you provide them with should have a protein content between 12-14% and should be as low in fat as possible.

The fattening types of sow nuts are designed for meat pigs and farm hogs. This type of pellet has a high protein content and is designed to make a pig put on weight as quickly as possible. This is why it is of critical importance that your pig is <u>not</u> fed this type of pig feed.

There are pig feeds specifically designed for Potbellied Pigs and pet pigs. These are the best type of feed you can buy for your pet. They have been specially designed to cater for a pet pig's dietary needs and nutritional requirements.

Dedicated Potbellied Pig feeds can sometimes be a bit harder to buy, they are often not as commercially available as the standard pig feeds. Manufacturers and brands vary from country to country. To find this type of feed in your country, try searching for the term 'Potbellied Pig feeds' on the Internet—this will give you a list of possible feeds and brands that are available in your country.

Vitamins & Minerals

A balanced diet is critical to the health of your pig. I recommend topping up your pig's food with a few of the following:

Add a children's multivitamin to their daily feed. Just make sure you use the correct dose for your pig—this should be the dose appropriate to a child of the same weight. You can try adding the tablet whole to the pig's feed to see if he eats it. If not, try crushing it up and sprinkling on their feed.

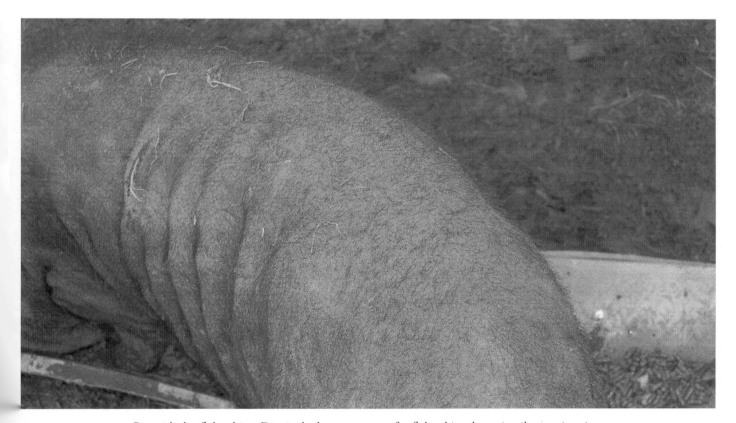

Pig with dry flaky skin - Diet is the best treatment for flaky skin, then pig oil or moisturizer

Cod liver oil can be added to their feed. It's great for joint health and a shiny coat. I personally prefer to use cod liver oil powder as you seem to waste less (although it's harder to find than the oil). We simply add a tablespoon of powder, per pig, to their daily food ration.

Flax seeds, linseed oil, or flax oil can also be used as a nutritional top up. These are often cheaper than cod liver oil and can sometimes be bought in bulk quantities–this is great if you have a few pigs. Even a tablespoon of olive oil can be used as a top up.

Feeding your pig dark, leafy, green vegetables is a great way to balance their diet and help promote good health. Dark greens are low in calories, and are high in fibre and water content. Frozen greens can be fed to pigs, as can 'off the shelf' (or old) veggies. Do not feed them mouldy veggies as this could cause them harm. Usually it's best to give them their greens as a second feed in the afternoon if possible. Do not feed them fruit, it's high in sugar and will cause them to become fat.

Pig Treats

Personally we recommend sticking with low-fat and low-sugar foodstuffs (i.e. carrots, cabbage, etc.) when it comes to treats.

We also recommend that you should keep the treats to a minimum and only provide them as a reward for good behaviour.

Always get something out of your pig before feeding them their treat–this might be something as simple as a head scratch, belly rub, a twirl. Making the pig work for their food in this way will prevent them from seeing you just as a food dispenser. It also helps the pig associate good behaviour with a reward.

Pig Behaviour and Food

You want to avoid your pet pig seeing you as nothing more than a giver of food and treats. Pigs can easily build up bad eating habits and behaviours if you give them the chance. If you constantly give into their demands for food, and give them everything they want, when they want it, you'll end up with a spoilt animal that is pushy and nightmare to keep.

Pigs are very intelligent animals and they will use all their brainpower to figure out ways of getting what they want, especially when it comes to food. They'll use noise, temper tantrums and squealing, if they think it will get them some extra food.

It's also very hard to reverse bad behaviour once it's present in your pig. Slowly, you'll need to try and reverse any bad habits they've built up and reduce the attraction to food–and believe me, they'll try to resist. It's possible to do, but you'll need to have lots of patience. You need to be determined to show them who's boss and who controls the food.

A pig will quite happily eat and scoff all day given the chance. This is where the phrase 'eat like a pig' comes from. Do not let your pig fall into this cycle of bad behaviour. Sticking to the correct diet is absolutely essential for your pet's health and makes things far easier for yourself.

Also, all pet pig keepers should make an effort to train their pig. Pig training isn't just there to make them perform tricks which are cool and funny, it also serves a purpose. Firstly, it establishes that you're the boss (more about this in the Behaviour section). Secondly, they realize they have to work for their food.

So try and make an effort to teach your pig a few basic tricks, because in the long run, it'll reduce the chance of them becoming a badly behaved, spoilt little pet. You won't regret it.

Making a Pig Lose Weight

Pigs put on weight very easily and it is extremely hard for them to lose it. Unlike a dog a pig cannot be easily persuaded to walk and exercise. They're very stubborn animals at the best of times; it's very hard to force them to do anything against their will, especially exercise.

If you are trying to make your pig lose weight then it is easier to attack their diet and slowly make the changes there. They will notice the change and you should be prepared for a fight, but this is an easier solution than trying to force them to exercise.

Keeping an obese animal is also expensive because you're just throwing unnecessary extra food down their necks. An obese animal has a higher risk of disease and health problems; this could mean additional vet's bills as you attempt to treat their weight problems. Bear this in mind the next time your pet pig is demanding food.

Food and exercise can be combined, to a degree, with the use of a feed ball/busy ball. A busy ball is a ball that you place food inside. Once the pig starts to knock and move the ball around, small amounts of food are released. The food placed inside needs to be a dried pellet or the ball won't operate properly. Similar devices are available for dogs and horses.

Brands and manufacturers vary depending on which country you live in; to find one in your country try searching for any of the following terms on the Internet or through Amazon: busy balls, horse feed ball, Likit horse feed ball, puppy treat ball. If you search for any of these, you'll find examples of the toy and what it does. The balls designed for horses are the best for pigs; they take more punishment than the puppy ones.

These are superb toys for pet pigs and will keep your pet busy and active for hours, they also have the added bonus of being a great boredom buster as well. Just remember to remove part of the pig's daily ration of sow nuts when using a feed ball. You do not want to be giving them any more extra pig nuts just because they're using a feed ball. We usually remove a third of their morning feed ration and place this in the feed ball to keep them busy.

Chapter 11 - Pigs, Laws and Movements

In this chapter we'll be covering how to transport your pigs, and how to help them settle into their new home. We'll also be touching on USA and UK law regarding the movement of pigs, and we'll offer a little advice for those of you who live in other countries.

Preparation is the key to making sure your piggy's transition to his/her new home is as smooth as possible. You should try to have as much of their stuff ready as possible.

Try to have at least the following ready for their arrival:

- Water bowl, bucket, or watering system

- Pig food – Non-fattening sow nuts or a dedicated Potbelly feed

- Bedding area – weather proof and filled with barley straw or towels

- Paddock/Field/Garden ready–make sure all fencing is secure and free from holes and gaps

Your Country's Pig Laws–Find Them Out

Every country has different rules and regulations regarding the movement and keeping of pigs. It would be impossible to cover them all in one book, so here's some general advice which should be followed, regardless of the country you live in:

Try using the Internet to find out how your country classifies pigs. Most countries will class pigs as livestock, therefore may be subject to similar rules that cows, sheep, and other meat producing animals, fall under. You'll probably have a government department that controls farming and agriculture; this is the first place to look.

Most government departments have their own website these days. Find the government department which regulates the farming and agriculture industry in your country and check their rules on pigs–specifically the rules and regulations concerning transporting and keeping them. Make notes of these and make sure you understand them.

Check yours with your local council, local government, and the people who control your local area or state. Make sure you find out if there are any laws that apply to you with regards to keeping pigs.

Check the tenancy agreement of your home, the deeds to your house or your housing contracts- sometimes a property can be subject to certain laws prohibiting the types of animals which can be kept on a property. Although this is pretty rare it's not completely unheard of.

If you know a person locally who keeps pigs, ask them. Don't trust their judgment one hundred percent, they might be wrong. But, they might be able to point you in the direction of the department where you can find out which rules do apply.

Find an Internet farming forum, specific to your country, and ask questions there.

This is a pretty good way of finding out what rules apply when keeping and moving pigs in your country. You might also be able to talk to people who are in the pig industry, people who deal with these laws on a daily basis; these are the best people to ask. Most importantly, they might be aware of any new legislation which has recently come into effect.

If you have neighbours, you must consider their feelings; tell them what you're planning to do. Where are you keeping your pigs? Is this land/property close to your neighbour's home? Will they mind the noise and squealing? Some pigs are noisy, some pigs aren't–make sure your neighbours are okay with you owning animals like this, animals that could possibly disturb them. The last thing you want is a dispute or even legal proceedings against your new pets.

UK Pig Movements and Law

CPH Number (UK Only)

In the UK pigs are classed as livestock, so they're subject to certain laws regarding their movements. Any person moving pigs must adhere to these, or you may face prosecution or a possible fine. Just because the pig you are keeping is a pet doesn't mean these laws don't apply to you.

Before you move any pig you must have a CPH (County Parish Holding) number for your premises or home. No legal transportation of pigs can take place between buyer and seller unless both addresses have a CPH number.

A CPH number can be obtained by calling the RPA (Rural Payments Agency) on the following number:

0845 603 7777

Their website and further details can be found using the link below:

http://goo.gl/MTqADe

The process of obtaining a CPH number is relatively simple. Once you've phoned them they will ask you a series of questions, they require you to provide some personal details such as your name and address. Once done, it takes around 1-2 weeks for your number to be processed and sent to you. There is a common misconception that you need to have your property inspected to obtain a CPH number, this is false.

Moving Pigs & UK Buyer and Seller requirements (UK Only)

In the UK, it's now the responsibility of the person who you're collecting the pigs from to update BPEX (British Pig Executive) about your animal's movement. You'll need to provide them with certain important details, such as: your CPH number, car registration number, address, transportation time, pig condition, and a few other pieces of information. Some of the information you are required to provide may seem odd. This is because BPEX movement records are designed to record the movement primarily of pigs in the pork industry, and not pet pigs.

If you are moving pigs to a different property, or land that has another CPH number, then it will be your responsibility to update the BPEX records.

BPEX details are:

Telephone: 0844 335 8400

The BPEX website:

http://www.eaml2.org.uk/ami/home.eb

I've always had difficulty using this system. It struggles when moving pigs to personal addresses (i.e. non-farm related addresses). If you're moving pigs from a property and you are struggling to enter the correct information into the online system, try phoning BPEX, they'll be able to submit your details manually into their system.

21 Day Standstill Period (UK Only)

When moving livestock in the UK there are certain procedures that must be followed; once you move pigs onto a property you cannot move them again for another 21 days. If you have other livestock on site, such as cows or sheep, you cannot move them either for seven days. If you ever move your pigs onto another property that has a different CPH number, BPEX will have to be notified via their website; this will trigger the 21 day standstill again.

Different types of livestock have different standstill periods. Check the Defra (Department for Environment, Food & Rural Affairs) website if this affects you.

Moving Pigs in the USA and Zoning

Zoning

You need to thoroughly research the Zoning and Home Owners' Association rules in your area. Many pig owners have ended up on the wrong side of them after they've bought a pig and taken it home. They've then had to endure the heartbreak and stress of officials trying to evict or remove their beloved pet. Make sure you research this thoroughly before you even consider buying a pig as a pet.

Each state in the USA has its own zoning laws; however, these are primarily aimed at larger livestock type animals. They sometimes do not cover animals which are kept as pets, such as pigs.

Every single town and city has different zoning regulations. And, within a single town, different areas can have their own particular zoning regulations.

Home Owners' Associations also have their own rules and regulations covering pets, their rules override any local rules. The Home Owners' Association has the last say on whether you can keep a pet pig on your property. If you get a 'yes pigs are allowed' from the zoning laws, and a 'no pigs are not allowed' from the Home Owners' Association, then you cannot keep any pigs. The Home Owners' Association ruling is final. The whole situation is a minefield and needs navigating with great care.

Here's some general advice:

• Make sure you get written copies of <u>both</u> the zoning ordinances for your area, and a written copy of any Home Owners' Association rules. Make sure you keep this paperwork safe.

• You'll need written copies of these documents incase you're ever challenged about your right to keep a pig.

• Do <u>not</u> rely on anyone's word or any verbal agreements regarding the Zoning and Home Owners' Association rules. You need written proof to contest any challenges - a verbal agreement (even if it's from a council official) won't stand up in court.

• Don't assume that council, government or local officials know the rules. There have been cases where a pig eviction has been attempted, even though (on paper) the owners were perfectly within their rights to keep pigs, according to the written Zoning laws.

Moving Pigs in the USA

The USDA (US Department of Agriculture) classes all pigs as livestock. There is no allowance made for pet pigs. Different states have different rules that affect pig movements. Make sure you find out how this affects you – speak with your vet about this and your planned route.

If you're crossing USA state lines your pig may need a health certificate and a permanent ID. In certain states you may also require an entry permit. Health certificates can take a few days to obtain, as can permits, so make sure you factor this into your movement plan. Again, it's advisable to speak to your local vet about your plans and route, hopefully they'll be able to provide you with the correct legal requirements when transporting your pet.

Please take the above as general guidelines about zoning and movements. The author of this book is from the UK and not the USA, so the above information has been put together from other books and websites found online. I have no direct experience with zoning regulations, so take my advice as a rough guide at the best.

If you're looking for an expert on pet pigs and zoning regulations, I suggest you checkout Becky DiNolfi's website. Her site address is below:

http://www.petpigzone.com/

Chapter 12 - The Journey Home

The size of pig you're moving will determine what transportation equipment will be required to move them. A metal dog cage (medium to large size) makes an excellent transportation cage for piglets. They're sturdy enough to resist your piglets' attempts to escape, and strong enough to hold them thrashing about if they become scared.

Make sure the floor of the cage is strong and secure. You don't want to lift your cage only to have the floor collapse under the weight of the piglets. The floor may have to take anything upwards of 20lbs in weight, possibly more. Check that it can bear this weight, before using it. Line your cage with straw or towels; this'll make the cage more comfortable and safer. The lining will provide extra grip for your piglets; it'll also help to soak up any poo or urine on the journey home.

If you are transporting piglets in the rear of a car it's a good idea to block the back windows out, as it can quickly turn into a greenhouse if the sun is shining into it.

Take care with your car's internal temperature–don't let your pig get too warm on your journey home. Make sure it is well ventilated and that there is air flowing around their cage. It might be worth also leaving the back windows open while you are travelling, to allow extra ventilation.

If you are travelling a long distance you should provide your pig with water. You may have to stop every few hours and let your pig drink from a bowl to keep them hydrated.

In some countries–when transporting livestock or pigs–you may need to log the time, place, and date of any stops you make. These may need to be submitted to a government, or official, department along with other paperwork. Please make sure you check your country's regulations on transporting pigs to make sure you adhere to any laws or requirements.

Piglets and adults are usually laid back when they are travelling. The hardest part, and the most stressful, is getting them into a cage or transporter. When you actually start to drive most pigs will lie down and fall asleep. Pigs usually find the motions and vibrations of the car quite relaxing, so much so that it can relax their bowls. Don't be surprised if you have a few bad smells coming from their cage or transporter. Usually you will find the odd bit of poo in their straw cage or transporter. Sometimes they will poo due to the stress of getting them into a cage or transporter, other times the vibrations of car can be the cause. Don't worry too much about this, if you find any lumps when you arrive home throw them in their potty area. This can be a good way of showing your pig where you want them to go potty.

Moving Adults Pigs

If you are moving larger animals or adult pigs, you may need the use of an animal (livestock) trailer, pick-up truck or a van. A trailer is probably the most common thing to use when transporting adult pigs. You can either buy, borrow or rent one.

If you're renting a trailer make sure to book it a few weeks in advance. Sometimes it can take a week or two for a trailer to become available so make sure you book it with plenty of time to spare, to avoid any problems.

The size of trailer you need will be determined by the number of pigs you are moving, and the size of the animals. Make sure you get an estimated size of each pig so you can obtain a trailer or vehicle of the correct size. Bear in mind, if you're using a trailer you will need a towing bar fitted to your vehicle.

If your journey takes more than a couple of hours, you'll need to provide your pig with water. In a trailer you can get away with sticking a large flat bucket in a corner, with a few bricks inside it (to help prevent it tipping) to provide water throughout the journey.

Make sure you keep an additional supply of water handy in case the water spills out of the bucket. The longer your journey, the hotter your climate, and the more pigs you are moving, the more water you'll need to have stored. An adult pig will need to drink around 3-6 litres of water per day depending on your climate. Use this rough guide to estimate how much you may need for your journey home.

Pigs are not sure-footed animals, it's easy for them to slip on metal flooring and possibly injure themselves. So, make sure your trailer is lined with straw, or some other soft material. It'll also provide your pigs with some extra comfort during the ride home.

If you're transporting pigs in a cold climate it is essential to fill the trailer with dry straw to help them keep warm.

Moving adult pigs into a trailer can be tricky. Pigs are stubborn animals to move at the best of times; moving them into a trailer can be a nightmare. The *carrot and stick* approach should always be the first method to try when moving pigs. It's easier to get a pig to follow you with a bucket of food (or pellets) than it is to force or direct them. Try shaking a bucket of food in front of them and let them have a sniff at it; this hopefully should encourage them to follow you into the trailer.

Sometimes throwing a few handfuls of pellets (or food) into the back of the trailer can spur the pig to move. Make sure they see you throw the food in though.

If this doesn't work you may have to use force. A pig board is recommended for this. Basically, a pig board is a piece of wood or plastic, roughly the width and height (or slightly bigger) than a pig. The board wants to be lightweight enough for you to be able to move it around quickly and easily. It also needs two holes in the top for handles–this makes moving the board much easier and quicker.

Pig boards can be bought if needed. They are frequently used in pig showing and in farmers' markets. If you fancy building your own, just search for the term *'pig board'* to get an idea of the size and shape of them. Below is a link to a Google image search which will show you a few examples:

http://goo.gl/LCklP1

Pigs usually try to run through you, and not around you. These boards will help you control the animal's direction and help prevent it from running through you. It takes a bit of practise and patience to be able to move a pig quickly with a pig board, but it's more effective than trying to stop them with your hands.

Very stubborn pigs may require two people (or more) to move them. Sometimes combining two pig boards and two people together is the best approach for a problem animal. Two pig boards can be combined in a wedge or wall shape; you can then effectively manoeuvre the pig in the required direction.

Just bear in mind that when a pig doesn't want to be moved it will dig its heels in, so be prepared for a bit of hard work and a struggle.

Mixing Pigs

Care needs to be taken when mixing new pigs together. You might be planning to get your current pet a new friend; or you may be thinking of adding a new pig to an existing herd.

Either way you need to be aware of a few things:

- Your pigs will fight when they first meet each other. It can be noisy and seem really vicious, so be prepared.

- An established herd (or the head of the herd) may not let the newcomer into their sty/shed for the first couple of nights, or even for the first few weeks. This is natural, it's just them asserting their dominance over each other.

- Old un-castrated males (breeding boars) should never be kept together or introduced, especially if they're of a similar height and size. Their attacks on each other will be extremely vicious, and they'll sometimes fight to the death. If you have boars of a breeding age keep them separate.

- When new pigs meet the fighting is inevitable, they have to establish who the top pig is. Usually the biggest one wins.

- Fighting will be worse between pigs of a similar size and weight. If you mix a small pig with a big pig the fighting will be over pretty quickly–the small pig will quickly learn where its place is in the herd, it won't pick a fight it has no chance of winning. If you mix a big pig with a small one, the big pig will likely take over the top spot.

- The fighting can last for a few days. Often the fighting is more traumatic for the owners than it is for the pigs.

- Unfortunately the only way to deal with the fighting is to let it play out and keep an eye on it. If a pig takes a serious injury then you will have to separate them. A few cuts and bruises are okay, but any torn ears or damaged eyes and you'll have to separate them.

Sometimes you may have to provide the new pig with a temporary home if the existing pig (or herd members) won't let them into their bed/sty/shed for the first few days.

When pigs fight, the ears are the most likely part of the pig to be damaged. One tip is to smear all the pigs' ears in Vaseline/petroleum jelly before mixing them. This makes the ears slippery and they're less likely to get torn.

Treat any wounds with an anti-septic cream or hydrogen peroxide. Pigs cannot lick their sides and backs, so creams can safely be used to treat these parts as they won't ingest them. Pigs can safely ingest hydrogen peroxide, so use this on the parts of their body that they can lick.

Chapter 13 - Once At Home

The First Few Days

Pigs don't like change, especially moving to a new home. Because of this your pig will be very scared, so we need to take steps to enable them to settle in as quickly as possible.

For the first few days you should isolate your piglet to a small space. If you're housing your pigs in a shed outside you may want to build a smaller perimeter fence around it. The pictures are an excellent illustration of this:

The fenced off area should be big enough to allow your pig to turn around easily. There should also be enough room for their food and water bowls, and enough room for them to go to the toilet. Pigs do not like to go potty near their food or water so make sure you place their food and water together, at one side of the pen.

Confining your pig to a small area allows them to quickly learn where their bed, water and food are. A pig will return to this area when they feel threatened, when they're scared, when they need to get out of the weather and when they want to rest.

Once they've established what their bed looks and smells like, you can let them explore the rest of their home. If they need to return to their bed or toilet in a hurry, they should have a better idea of where it is, now that they are familiar with that area.

Isolating your pig to a small area for the first few days is especially important if the pig has a very large area (such as a field, forest, paddock) to play in. The bigger their area is, the easier it is for the pig to get lost–this means a higher chance of you having to move the pig manually back to their home until they get used to the layout.

During the first few days keep the noise and new visitors down to a minimum. There will be lots of new noises, smells, and faces at the new home, it'll be enough for the pig to have to deal with these, you don't want to add anymore to the mix. Also, you want the pig to bond with you. The pig should see and hear you the most as you're their new owner.

During this time you want the pig to get used to you being around them. This wants to be at the pig's pace, not yours. Don't try and force the pig to come to you; don't try to picking your pig up straight away; if you do this you'll risk scaring the pig even further.

Try sitting in their pen and letting them come up to you–let them investigate you, let them sniff you. Pigs respond well to your tone of voice, so talk to them in a warm and friendly manner. Offer them your hand and let them sniff it, though be careful as young piglets are prone to biting and they do have very sharp teeth.

If your pig is happy with your hands being placed near them, try to touch them and give them a scratch. If your pig is coping well, and allowing you to touch or pat them, reward their good behaviour with a treat (a piece of carrot or a grape).

Don't rush to try and get the pig used to you and to be tame. They will come around pretty quickly if you follow the above steps. Remember, your pet may live to be 20 years old, so you have plenty of time to get used to each other.

Just remember that treats are a reward for good behaviour. But, after the pig has settled in, you should minimise the treats, they shouldn't be given to your pig every time they see you. You don't want your pig to view you as nothing more than a food dispenser. Once your piglet is getting familiar with you, reward them randomly after any good behaviour.

You do not want the pig to think they will be getting a treat every time they are good, or after you've petted them, this could lead to the pig becoming badly behaved and demanding. A scratch, a stroke, or a pat on the head should be enough of a reward for your pet when they've been good.

A perfect pig setup for a garden. Notice the use of strong fencing which will easily be able to hold an adult. Bark chippings have been added to the floor to aid drainage and minimize muddy conditions during the wetter parts of the year.

The flagged floor at the entrance to the shed will help wear down the pigs hooves naturally. The door of the shed has been split into two - this allows the top door to be shut during bad weather.

Photo above: plenty of bedding straw and will ensure the pig is warm and comfy when sleeping and resting

Introducing Other Pets

Pigs get on fine with other animals. We've seen our own pigs get along with, dogs, cats, chickens, sheep, and even the occasional rabbit on our farm. If the pigs are kept in a pair or more you usually find they tend to ignore any other animals that are about and pose no threat to them.

One piece of advice I can offer, regarding mixing all other animals and pigs is; don't feed them all in the same area at the same time. Pigs usually like their daily feed to themselves and can get upset if another animal or pet attempts to eat it. Show them courtesy and feed your other animals somewhere else or at a different time.

Be careful if your pig mixes with larger animals such as cattle or horses, especially around feeding times. It's quite easy for your pig to get kicked and injured. Pigs are fast learners, they'll quickly figure out when you're feeding the other animals, and they'll try to steal their food if given a chance.

It might be worth keeping your pigs locked, or fenced in, until your other animals are fed, to avoid any conflict.

Also, pigs shouldn't be allowed to eat feeds designed for other animals and vice-versa. Pig food is specifically made for pigs just as dog food is specifically made for dogs. Animal feeds can have minerals and nutrients which should only be fed to a specific animal–feeding them to other animals may make the animals ill and could be illegal. The only exception to this–as discussed in the Feeding Your Pig chapter–is where certain types of horse feed would be an acceptable substitute for pig feed.

Some feeds are designed to make animals put on weight as quickly as possible, try to avoid your pig accessing them. They could easily cause your pig to become fat over time, they may also develop a sweet tooth for these types of feed and start to ignore their own pig food–this is something you really want to avoid.

Dogs and Pigs

Do pigs get along with dogs? The answer is <u>yes</u> and <u>no.</u> Pigs are a dog's natural prey. In the wild they would be part of a dog packs' regular food. Because of the dogs' natural instinct to hunt pigs, you should never leave the two alone unsupervised.

A lot of this depends on the temperament of the dog. If you have owned your dog for a while you should have a good idea of its character, and whether or not the dog can be trusted. So it is your decision to make, use your judgment, and don't rush into things.

If you are introducing your dog to your pig, do it by sight only at first: don't let them come into physical contact straight away, do this for the first few days. They need to get used to the smell of each other and also get used to the sounds each animal makes.

When you do let them have physical contact make sure you have the dog on a leash, so it can be controlled. You need to be able to remove the dog quickly if it starts to play up.

Never leave a dog and pig together unsupervised. You need to be 100% certain that the animals can be trusted with each other and this might take months of evaluation and supervision on your part.

Even then I wouldn't ever leave them together unsupervised for long periods of time.

Never let a pack of dogs near a pig. Their pack instinct is much stronger when there's more than one of them, they're far more likely to attack and cause a serious injury as a pack.

Be very careful when mixing smaller piglets and dogs. The smaller the pig, the greater the chance your dog may attack them.

Pigs and Small Children

Small piglets are usually fine around young children. If the children are noisy they could startle the animal, so try to keep things as quiet as possible.

Care needs to be taken when children are feeding piglets. Piglets, like puppies, usually don't know how to take food correctly out of a person's hand. They may try to snatch food from a hand, sometimes they can accidentally bite fingers; pigs have very sharp teeth that can easily break through the skin.

Try to keep your hands and fingers as far away as possible from their mouths when feeding them. If you're allowing a child to feed a piglet I highly recommend using whole carrots. Feeding your piglet something long like this allows you to keep fingers a safe distance from the pig's mouth. This way, if the piglet does try to snatch, your hand should hopefully be out of the way.

Adult Pigs and Small Children

Care also needs to be taken if you own an adult pig and you have small children around.

An adult pig can easily knock a child down to the ground. Also, pigs can run quite fast—especially when there's food involved. You don't want your adult pig to come running, barging your child out of the way, because they think it's their dinner time. So be careful, and use your common sense when it comes to pigs and small children.

It's worth noting though that adult pigs tend to take things out of your hand more gently than a piglet. However, even if your pig does possess this skill, I would still try to feed them long treats (carrot, celery sticks, etc.), rather than feeding them things from the palm of your hand. You really want to avoid those sharp teeth, they can cause a nasty nip.

Chapter 14 - Potty Training

Personally, I feel the best way to keep pet pigs is: outside; in a pair; in a large garden or paddock; using a weather proof shed (full of straw) as their home. Keeping pigs outside is by far the easiest way. A pair of pigs, kept outside, are a self-contained entity; they require less care and are less dependent on humans. They have each other, the ability to graze, and other outdoor stimuli–the chance of them becoming bored is greatly reduced. Remember, a bored pig is more likely to be a problem, and more likely to cause damage to your property.

For some people keeping a pig in their house is the only option–especially for those who live in cold climates, and those who lack sufficient outdoor space. Keeping a pet pig inside was fairly widespread during the original pot belly craze back in the late eighties and early nineties, and it's still quite common today.

I would say that indoor pigs are far more common in the USA than in the UK. Keeping a pig inside brings its own problems and demands; certain challenges have to be met if things are to run smoothly. Potty training is definitely one of them!

If you plan to keep your pig indoors permanently you must have around sixty square feet of space for the pig to play in, this should also be on a single floor (single storey house). A house with a second floor (two or more storeys) doesn't count: pigs shouldn't be made to walk up and down stairs–it's very bad for their joints, especially adult pigs.

Two Types of Potty Training

There are basically two types of potty training, these are when:

1. The pig is kept permanently indoors and it goes to the toilet indoors.

2. The pig is kept mainly inside the house but goes to the toilet outside (partial potty training).

Each requires a slightly different approach when it comes to training your pet. Even if you are planning to let your pig go outside to potty I would still recommend keeping a potty area inside your home. Piglets cannot hold their bladders well until they are around two years old, so, for this reason, a partial potty training solution must be considered.

Your pig will need to go to the toilet during the night, and at other times when there is no one around to let them out. So even if your pig has some outdoor access, a degree of potty training will be required.

Your circumstances and your home environment play a key role in the decision to keep your pig inside or outdoors. If you are at work for eight hours a day (or something similar) then you cannot keep a pig cooped up in a house–it would cruel, and the pig will probably cause damage to due to boredom and loneliness.

Also, if you're away from the pig for extended periods, it makes the first type of potty training practically impossible.

If you're away from your home for long periods your pig will need to be kept outside with enough room and enough stimuli (toys, things to graze on, etc.). You will need to make an effort to keep it busy and entertained.

If you are fortunate enough to have a very large house, and you are at home for most of the day, then it is possible to keep a pig indoors and potty train them.

An important point to note is this–if you plan to keep a female indoors permanently, or keep them indoors at night, you must have them spayed. An un-spayed female is impossible to potty train. When an un-spayed sow comes into heat she'll urinate anywhere (it's one of the ways she attracts a boar). Every three weeks you'll have to deal with this behaviour if she's left un-spayed.

Male pigs should be castrated regardless of whether they're being kept inside or out; but you knew this already didn't you? The only exception to this rule is if you are planning to breed from the boar, in which case he should be kept outside in his own dedicated area (more on this in the Breeding section, later in the book). Never keep a breeding pig inside in a house–you are asking for trouble (and that's an understatement).

Once they reach sexual maturity intact males stink! The smell they produce is designed to attract any nearby females who are in heat. Unfortunately, it's only female pigs who like this smell and not us humans.

Getting Started

Potty training a pig is difficult. It takes persistence and it takes patience, on your part and your pig's. It can take up to twelve months to properly potty train a pig.

Also, it's common for pigs to relapse during training. If this happens you may have to restart their training from scratch. This is one of main reasons I prefer to keep my pigs outdoors. Anyway, enough talk; let's get on with how we actually train them.

Potty training starts as soon as the piglets are born. When a piglet is old enough to walk they will move to the side of their nest area to defecate. All the piglets in the nest use their excellent sense of smell to find the correct place to go potty. Once a spot has been picked, they'll all sniff out this place when they need to go.

Once the piglets are a bit older they will usually choose to poo in the same place as the sows, during the farrowing, usually this is as far away from their bedding and watering area as possible. Once the piglet has been fully weaned and moved to a new home the next stage of potty training can begin.

A young piglet will need to potty very often, usually once every 1-2 hours. A year old pig should be able to keep their bladder controlled for around 4 -5 hours. A 2-3 year old pig should be able to control their bladder very well and should also be able to hold their urine for 12 hours or more.

As discussed in the previous chapter it is imperative that your piglet is isolated to a small space during their first week or so. If you are keeping your pig indoors a garage or large laundry room can be used for this.

For pigs kept outside, a small pen should be placed around their sty/shed. You should give the pig enough room for them to have an area to sleep; an area for their food and water; and an area for their litter box.

The litter box wants to be approximately 3ft x 3ft (maybe larger if your pig is on the big side). You could start off with a smaller sized box for a piglet, but you'll have to alter it as the piglet grows bigger.

The basic rule of thumb regarding litter box size is this–the pig should have enough room to be able to turn around easily. Use a box which is too small and your pig will be reluctant to use it, and he may choose to potty elsewhere.

The litter box should be easy for the pig to get in and out off. Pigs do not like to step up when going to the toilet, so make sure the box has low sides. Your pig should easily be able to step in and out of the box.

The box should also have a non-slip floor; otherwise the pig will be reluctant to use it. A rubber mat cut to size and placed in the bottom makes an excellent non-slip surface.

Do not use cat litter, or clay pellets, as litter for your pig. Pigs will often eat these and the results can be fatal. Pine shavings, paper pellets or old towels will work just as well. If you choose to use old towels just make sure you replace or wash them every few days, this will help prevent any bad odours.

Also, make sure you keep the box as clean as you can. The odd bit of poo in the box is okay and this should encourage them to use it but don't let the waste build up too much or your pig will choose to potty somewhere cleaner.

All these things need to be done before you bring your pig home. You do not want to be moving things around, adding litter trays, and changing things once your pig has arrived. When he gets to his new home he'll be scared, changing things around won't help him settle.

Young Piglets

If you are dealing with young piglets, place the litter box fairly close to their bed (try to keep it away from the feeding and watering area though). Young piglets will need to go to the toilet frequently, so the less steps they have to take the better–they'll learn more quickly.

Once the piglet has got the hang of things you can start to move the box away from their bed. Some pigs won't like their potty box anywhere near their bed or feeding area, try moving their potty box away from these areas if they won't use it. Once they get used to using the box you can begin the process of steadily moving it further away from their bed and feeding areas.

Starting the Training

The chances are that when your pig has been brought to your home they'll have pooed in their transportation cage or crate (this might be a trailer if you are moving an adult). Pick up a few pieces of poo and place them in their litter box. This should encourage the pig to use the designated potty area when the time comes.

During the first few days of arrival you'll be attempting to get to know your pet. Sit in with them; talk to them; scratch them and pet them. If you catch him going to the potty area, and doing his business in the right spot, praise him and make a fuss. The pig needs to be told he's doing the right thing. Try to avoid giving him treats every time he uses the potty in the correct way; the pig may quickly cotton on that if he poos he gets fed; this could be a slippery slope to more problems further down the line.

Any stray pieces of faeces should be moved to their litter box. Again, this will help train the pig where they need to go and do their business.

The pig should stay in this confined area, with their litter box, until there are no stray accidents. Once the pig gets the idea, you can start to let them out into the other part of your home.

Never leave a piglet out of their litter box area for more than an hour, they simply cannot hold their bladder long enough; return them frequently and allow them to use the potty.

Harness training your pig can make the task of moving them to their litter box much easier (harness training is covered in the Behaviour section, later in the book).

Ensure your piglet uses the potty: before they go out to play; after a nap; and after they have eaten anything. The trick is to keep your piglet's bladder as empty as possible thereby minimising the risk of him having any accidents in unwanted spots.

Once you have taken your piglet back to their box, issue the potty command–tell them to *"toilet"*, or *"go potty"* etc. Once they have done their business give them lots of praise for being a good pig. Over time your pet will learn this command; this should make the whole process of taking them back to their litter box to pee/poo far quicker.

For indoor pigs you may have to keep up the task of "hourly returns" to their litter box for anything up to six months. As stated earlier, patience and persistence are the keys to success. Some pigs will naturally return to their potty area more quickly than others. Even when your pig appears to be doing well, be prepared for the odd relapse; also be prepared for the pig to push the boundaries, they'll try other spots around your home where they can potty.

Partial Potty Training

Letting your Pig go outdoors

Piglets that have access to outdoor space may suddenly choose to start doing their business outside. This is fine; it's perfectly natural for a pig to prefer doing their business outdoors. The smell of the earth, the grass, and the leaves can naturally stimulate their bowels.

You'll probably find that your pig will pick a spot outside and then stick to it. If you do not like this spot simply keep moving his faeces to a different place; again, this should encourage your pet to change their toilet area.

You may still need their litter box in place for the times when your pig cannot get outside (during the night and when you are not at home).

Some pigs become agitated and noisy when they need to go outside; this can sometimes be a sign that they need the toilet.

Pigs that go outside to the toilet can be taught to give you a signal when they need to go. I've heard of one person teaching their pig to pull a rope with a bell on it, signalling when they need to go. Choose a signal which is right for you and your home.

Fitting a large dog door (large cat-flap style door) to the entrance of your home can be one solution to give your pig easy access to outside, when needed. If you fit something like this just make sure that it's not a security issue for your house. You wouldn't want a burglar or an intruder to use this door to gain access to your home, please take this into consideration.

In colder climates, or in winter, some pigs may be reluctant to leave the house to go to the toilet. You can make a few changes to help encourage piggy to go. Firstly, try and make sure their potty is as close to your house as possible–the quicker your pig can reach this area the better. Secondly, make sure their spot is sheltered and out of the wind.

Building a roof and some walls around his toilet spot can help. If your pig can get to his spot quickly, while not being blasted by wind, rain or snow, you stand a better chance of them wanting to go outside when the time comes.

Dealing with Accidents and Relapses

It is common for pigs to have a relapse later on in their training. Sometimes the owners have been training the pig for months, then the pig will find a new potty spot, and stick to it! The owner keeps trying to prevent their pet from going there, but nothing seems to work.

Two things can be happening here:

1. The piglet has always been going to this spot and taking a wee there, he's possibly been using this spot for a long time without you ever knowing. When he was very small the amount of urine he deposited there was too small to be noticed, however, as the pig has grown this patch suddenly becomes noticeable to their owner.

2. The pig has simply chosen a new spot to do his mess in. He or she likes this new indoor spot more than their potty.

The first thing you must do is properly eliminate the smell from the area. You need to clean the accident spot (or spots) with a cleaner designed to eliminate animal odours. The smell of the pig's urine will keep drawing them back to the same spot, it's very important you use a good quality cleaner to eliminate any smells.

If this doesn't solve the problem then try moving a heavy object over the spot. You could try rearranging your furniture to cover the accident areas. Your aim is to prevent the pig from getting to their new, favourite potty spot.

If you cannot cover the affected areas with anything heavy, and your pig is still using these spots when your back is turned, you could try setting up some sort of alert. A set of wind chimes hanging very low to the floor (low enough for your pig to bump into) could help notify you when piggy is sneaking off to their new spot. A couple of boxes of ringing balls could also do the same job, and alert you when piggy is up to no good.

If you hear a noise, you can hopefully catch them before they use the toilet. If you catch them in time, take them to their correct potty box as quickly as possible. If you caught them too late, or caught them in the act, you'll have to chastise them—tell them off and confine them to their sleeping quarters for a few hours as punishment.

You could try feeding your pig on their new favourite potty spot. Pigs don't like to do their business where they eat. This can sometimes change a bad habit.

Remember, pigs are quick learners and they have great memories, but they unlearn very slowly. It may take time to break any bad habits they pick up, so be prepared.

Chapter 15 - Behaviour and Training

Controlling your pig's behaviour can mean the difference between having a pet that is a real pleasure to keep, and owning a pet from hell. A basic understanding of their behaviour will really make your life (and your pet's) easier.

Pigs are very independent and intelligent animals, they believe they don't need you in order to survive. It's critical from the start you show them who is the boss, but this shouldn't be done through physical force, or hitting them.

Pigs are stubborn animals, it is very hard to force them to do anything, it is usually easier and more productive to encourage them to do the things you want.

Pig behaviour and psychology could fill its own book alone; it's far bigger than the scope of this book. If you're after a complete guide to pet pig behaviour, I recommend that you read Pricilla Valentine's book on the subject. She's one of the leading authorities on pet pig psychology in the world.

Her book can be found using the link below:

http://goo.gl/AysIFL

Keeping pigs outside rather than in a house does make things easier when it comes to controlling them. If they have the correct environment (outdoor space, an area to graze, secure fencing, boredom busting devices) sometimes only minimal training is required.

However, if you intend to allow your pig access to your home then training will be required to prevent problems. Remember, if you're keeping a female indoors, you must get her spayed otherwise you won't be able to train her.

Training pigs serves three main purposes:

1. Firstly, it establishes you as the boss of the herd. This is very important, especially once the pig reaches two years of age. At this age your pig will try to assert their dominance over the rest of the herd (this includes you and your family).

2. Secondly, it helps to minimise any bad behaviour your pig has around food.

3. Lastly, your pig realises it has to work for any treats. It cannot simply demand them from you.

Pig Aggression

Pig aggression can be due to various reasons. The pig might have a negative attachment to food, they may also be at an age where they are trying to assert their dominance over the herd, or they may have been mistreated by their previous owner. If the pig has aggressive tendencies they might not be safe around your family, especially children. You may have to change things in your home to help deal with these behavioural problems.

Some precautions to take are:

• Keep the pig away from very small children, separate them to a room or pen if needed

• If a pig charges you and tries to bite, put your hand on their forehead and push hard. This is hard to do with a piglet and can be terrifying with a large pig, but it does allow you to keep them at arm's length. After a moment or two your pig should step back and calm down. Keep repeating this if needed. In extreme cases a dustbin lid or a pig board can be used to shove back a really aggressive animal.

• If a pig is picking on certain family members but not others, then the pig is asserting their dominance over what he sees as the weaker members of the herd. I would recommend that the person who's being picked on feed the pig for a week and no one else. If the pig charges they should use the 'hand on forehead' technique to subdue the pig. Also, the pig must receive no food until they behave and submit to the person who's feeding them. It's critical that the person who is being attacked asserts their dominance over the pig otherwise the situation will never change.

• If your pig is attacking house guests then you should either keep them separate, or get your guest to use the 'hand on forehead' technique. Get the guest to give the pig a treat once they have been subdued and they are behaving correctly towards them.

• Never give into a pushy pig's demands. If they think they are in charge things will get far worse.

If you're going down the rescue pig route, it's a good idea to get your animal from a dedicated pig sanctuary. A good sanctuary will know their animals' behaviour and they should be able to match it to your circumstances.

The Way a Pig Sees the World

Pigs see the world as a ladder. Everyone in their herd is on that ladder, and you are part of that herd. It's very important you (and your family) are at the top of that ladder, otherwise you can expect trouble.

Pigs will try to assert their dominance through various kinds of behaviour; these may be: being noisy, aggressive or having temper tantrums. They're clever animals and they'll try different things, with different herd members, if it means they move up the ladder.

Do not tolerate any bad behaviour from your pig as it will become worse if left unchecked. Make sure you discipline them if they're bad (see below section for details).

The Terrible Twos

A pig is fully mature, emotionally, at around two years of age. At this time the pig will try to assert their dominance over the rest of the herd. It's not unusual for a well behaved piglet to turn into a brat at this age. At around two years they'll try to test you to see who has control—don't let them win.

Again, make sure you discipline them when they're playing up.

Also, teaching your pig a few tricks, when they're young, really helps to curb any bad behaviour once they reach the terrible twos.

Harness training

Harness training is a useful thing to teach your pig. It's especially important for a pig being kept inside, as it aids potty training.

If your pig is kept outside then you may never need to harness train them. It certainly does make moving them around, and visiting the vet, easier if you do train them.

If you're planning to buy a harness make sure you buy one designed specifically for pigs. A dog harness will easily slip off a pig, they simply aren't designed for their shape and size.

The best harnesses have a 'figure 8' that slips under the pig and fastens over their back. Make sure to measure your pig and buy the correct size harness. A harness which is too loose is useless, one which is too tight will make your pig uncomfortable.

Pigs do not like to stick their heads through loops or collars, so avoid harnesses of this type.

A quick search on the Internet for the term 'pig harness' should find stockists in your country.

How to Harness Train

It's far easier to harness train a young pig than it is an adult. When you clip a harness and lead to any pig for the first time they'll freak out. In the wild, pigs are only restrained when a predator has hold of them, so they'll naturally fight when this happens to them. It's far easier to hold a 10lb piglet when it throws a fit, holding onto an 80lb adult pig when it's freaking out is a tough job–this highlights the importance of starting them young. Also, once a pig has been trained to use a harness, they'll never forget–even if it's years later.

Your first task is to get your pig used to wearing their harness. Try slipping it on when they're eating, or when you're giving them a scratch, or when they're on your lap. Let them wear the harness as much as possible, leave it on for most of the day. Ideally you should attach the lead to the harness, this allows them to get used to the sensation of being clipped in.

Once the pig is accustomed to the harness, and being clipped in, you can now try using the lead. Again, they'll freak out the first few times they reach the end of it, but keep persisting, they'll soon get used to the sensation. The lead is your way of communicating with your pig. It's the way you'll direct and coax your pig to the place you want. After a few days of this they should become easier to handle.

Good Habits from the Start

Try to foster good habits from the start with your pet. Breaking bad habits later in their life is always more difficult than training them while they're young. Pigs have great memories; they learn very quickly and forget very slowly.

Don't encourage the piglet to do things that you wouldn't want an adult pig to do. If you don't fancy an adult pig sleeping in your bed, sitting on your sofa, etc. then exclude your piglet from such behaviour from the very beginning.

Don't fall into the trap of letting them do something because it's looks cute, remember your pig is going to grow. What seems cute now may be a pain in the backside to deal with once the animal is bigger.

Food

In the feeding section, earlier in the book, we discussed a few basic principles. As we know, pigs are very clever animals and they love their food. They'll use their brainpower to figure out ways of getting more food from you at every opportunity. Don't let them! When it comes to food make sure you get into good habits from the start.

Here are some tips:

- Feed your pig twice a day–sow nuts or pig pellets in the morning, dark leafy green veggies (or treats) in the afternoon.

- Always make them work for any extra food treats you give them–this is to prevent them seeing you as nothing more than a feed dispenser. A reward is for a good day's work, they need to learn this.

- Stick to the correct diet–make sure you feed them non-fattening sow nuts and keep the treats to a minimum. Veggies are best as they're low in sugar (mine love carrots and they can be bought quite cheaply from horse feed/equipment suppliers).

- If you have two, or more, pigs it's possible they will need to be fed using separate dishes to prevent fighting. Pigs can be quite vicious where food's concerned.

- Don't get into the habit of simply feeding your pet to quell their boredom; this is a slippery slope to disaster and will create a pushy pet.

Boredom

A bored pig is not a happy pig. Boredom in swine is one of the major causes of problems for pet pig owners–a bored pig can be noisy, annoying and destructive. In the feeding section we mentioned that boredom can be alleviated with the use of hay and silage. However, there are additional things you do to help reduce your pet becoming bored.

Remember your pig is your responsibility. It's up to you to provide them with things to do and prevent them from becoming bored.

Pair of Pigs

Keeping pigs in a pair or more is the best way to minimise boredom. Pigs are a herd animal and keeping them with one of their own kind is the best way to prevent boredom and loneliness.

I have often found that it's far easier to keep a pair of pigs than a single pig on its own. A single pig will require more work -you will need to provide it with more toys, more attention and more stimuli.

Two pigs together will happily keep each other company, and they will be quite content pottering about, grazing together, especially if they have the space.

Pig Toys

Toys can be used to keep your piggy's mind busy. I've used squeaky dog toys, old telephone directories, newspapers and footballs to keep my pigs occupied. The best toys I've found, to alleviate boredom, are feed balls. You may have come across these; they are used routinely with puppies and dogs. Feed balls work by placing a small amount of dry feed (usually sow nuts) inside the ball, when the pig knocks the ball around on the ground small amounts of food are released from small holes in the ball. These types of ball can keep a pig occupied for hours, they really do help in combating boredom, and they can also be used to help prevent a pig from rooting. They also provide great exercise as well. It is a good idea to take away part of their daily feed ration and place it into the ball rather than feeding them additional food. I recommend feed balls that are designed to be used with horses, they are usually heavy duty and robust enough to take a lot of punishment. For small piglets a puppy feed ball is usually best (until they get bigger then move on to the horse-sized feed ball).

Two brand names you might want to search the Internet for, to give you an idea of the type, are: 'Likit – Snak-a-Ball' & ''Horse Busy Ball'. Here's a link to one of the manufacturers, this should give you an idea of what they look like:

http://goo.gl/qXRrUL

A cheap version of these toys can be made by placing the dry food into a two litre, plastic drink bottle and poking two holes in the bottom of it. You simply replace the lid and give it to the pig.

Rooting Box

Another option to keep your pig occupied is to create a boredom box. This is a box roughly 2' x 3' wide with 6" high sides. Cover the bottom of the box with 2–3 inches of river rocks (you can get these from garden centres and nurseries). You can also add tennis balls, old shoes, dog toys and anything else you can think of. Don't add very large or sharp rocks, you run the risk of injuring your pig when they are moving things around. You can then hide treats in the box and let your piggy try to find them. Your pig will have to push around the rocks to find the treats hidden amongst the stones and toys. A box like this can keep a pig entertained for hours.

Discipline

If you follow the above points there is a good chance that you should be well on your way to owning a well-behaved pet pig.

However, from time-to-time you may need to discipline your pet. Pigs respond well to a strong firm voice and hand commands. Holding out a raised open hand and shouting '**no**' in a firm voice can stop them in their tracks. You might just need to keep on repeating this until they stop the bad behaviour.

A water pistol or something similar can be a great discipline tool as well. When piggy's behaving badly or got his head in something he shouldn't have, then give a quick squirt. They don't like it, and they will be annoyed at you, but it's an effective way to keep them out of trouble.

Another, more controversial, way to discipline your pig is to give them a short, sharp tap on the nose, and in a firm voice tell them '**no**'.

You should **never** hit or hurt your pig. Doing so might cause them to stop trusting you, and even liking you.

With my own pigs the first technique has always worked fine. Usually a pig will respond well to noise and hand gestures. I recommend trying this first before trying any of the others.

Pig Tricks

Pigs can be taught how to perform a variety of tricks, these include: sitting down, shaking paws (or hooves in the case of the pig), spinning around, and even, in extreme cases, they have been taught to ride a skateboard!

The simplest tricks to teach your pig are the spin or twirl. To do this:

1. Give her a treat.

2. Hold a second treat just above her nose and make her turn in a circle, whilst saying a cue word (either 'spin' or 'twirl' or any word you like).

3. If they do the trick correctly pat them on the head, tell them how good they are, and give them their reward.

Don't underestimate the value of teaching your pig a simple trick like this. Just teaching them one simple trick can be one of the best ways to curb potentially bad behaviour. It also helps both pig and person to learn how to communicate. Tricks also have the benefit of establishing you as the boss of the herd, and this is very important.

Chapter 16 - Pig Health

Pigs become ill, just like human beings—knowing what constitutes a healthy or sick animal will allow you to determine whether or not your pig is ill.

You should make an effort to spend time with your pig (or herd) as much as possible. Make sure you take note of your animal's normal behaviour on any normal day. Try to observe them and their little quirks; get to know their personality and patterns of behaviour. Being able to spot when your pig's not itself, or acting out of character, will help with diagnosing any problems when they arise.

I will stress that it is **very important** that you find yourself a vet who is familiar with livestock, especially pigs. Your regular vet, who treats your dog, cat, gerbil, etc. may not be familiar with livestock and pigs. You might find that you have to use a different veterinary surgery than your usual one.

Depending on where you live and where/how your pigs are kept—will determine the preventative measures or treatments your pig may need. If you only keep a single pig, in a house, in a suburb then the chances of your animal needing vaccinations or picking up a serious illness is greatly reduced (please note your local community guidelines may require you to vaccinate, this needs to be checked out first).

If you have had your pigs for a while and they never come into contact with other pigs then the risk of disease is going to be small. However, if your pigs come into contact regularly with other farm pigs, or you are frequently moving your pigs (or other livestock) on and off your land, then the risk of disease increases.

Pigs can also be carriers of disease, so just because the healthy pig you brought home looks fine, this doesn't mean it isn't carrying an infection or disease. The point I'm trying to make is this—owning a small quantity of pigs doesn't make you immune to illness and disease; it simply reduces the risk of transmission.

Viruses, bacteria, and other parasites can be carried on clothes and skin. Contagions can be picked up anywhere there are other pigs and livestock—this means that places such as: country shows/fairs, other pig farms, petting zoos, anywhere there is livestock are all possible places where infections can be picked up. Birds can also fly onto your property and have the risk of potentially depositing contagions. Although the risks are small they are still there.

Personally, when it comes to small-scale pig keeping, or just keeping pigs as pets, it's far easier to just be aware of what constitutes a healthy animal. If your pet starts acting abnormally or looking ill then it's far safer to call the vet and get an expert opinion. It is very easy to misdiagnose pig diseases and therefore apply the wrong treatment.

Pigs can suffer from hundreds of different diseases and sicknesses. To cover them all would need a full book in itself and would probably cause more confusion than understanding. Because of this I want to simply outline the basics that every novice pig keeper should be aware of.

The advice I offer is this:

- Contact your local vet, preferably one who deals with livestock—they'll have a better idea of the threats in your area and what preventative steps you need to take for your pigs

- Check your local community guidelines (depending on the country you live in this may, or may not, apply to you). Some guidelines require all pets in an area to be vaccinated against certain diseases.

- When diagnosing illnesses, the golden rule I, and other pig keepers, follow is this—if in doubt call the vet.

It's far too easy to make a wrong diagnosis, especially for a novice.

If you do want to research pig diseases I would suggest Googling the term. The pigsite.com has some excellent and in-depth articles on pig diseases and swine health.

Diagnosing Problems

Diagnosis starts with looking for behaviour that appears out of the ordinary, or out of place. Things to watch out for are:

- Is your pig off their food? Pigs never usually miss their feeding time, and are always hungry. If your pig is off his food this could mean something is wrong.

- Is your pig coughing and wheezing, or sneezing?

- How is your pig's posture? Is it hunched over?

- Is your pig shivering?

- Is your pig struggling to stand? Does your pig prefer to lie down? Does your pig look weak?

- Does their skin look okay? Does it look sore or red? Is there anything oozing from the skin?

An awareness of the above points could help indicate your pig is suffering from something.

If your observations seem to indicate that your pet is ill call a vet. It is always best to call an expert and describe the symptoms your pet is suffering from—this could mean the difference between life and death for your pet.

It's better to do this than to misdiagnose your pet's ailments and treat them incorrectly.

Vaccinations

Where you live, and how you're planning to keep your pig, will determine whether you need to vaccinate your or not.

The only certain question you should ask concerning vaccination is—does your country, state, county or local community have legal guidelines requiring you to vaccinate? You need to check this out—speak with your local vet regarding the vaccination requirements in your country and area.

If your pig is being kept indoors, or in a suburban or an urban area, and your community guidelines do not require it, and your vet says your pig is healthy—you have no real need to vaccinate.

If you are keeping your pig outside, you are planning to breed or you have pig farms in the area then you may need to vaccinate. Again, speak with your vet about the subject. They'll know the local area, its requirements, and the possible health threats out there.

If there are threats present in your area, and your vet recommends certain vaccinations, then you have a moral obligation (and maybe a legal requirement) to vaccinate your pig. Just because your pig is a pet doesn't mean you are exempt.

Rabies

Depending on the country you live in, and your community guidelines, the law may require all pets to have the rabies vaccination. If this applies to your area you will have to vaccinate your pig against rabies.

There is no rabies vaccination designed for specifically for pigs. Usually a vet will administer the same vaccination used for a dog.

All animals can get rabies, but pigs are particularly resistant to it. Usually the carriers of the disease are feral animals which have been infected (stray dogs, skunks, coyotes). Pigs will usually contract the disease from a feral animal through a bite or other contact, but it's usually very rare. If your pig is unlucky enough to get the disease isolate the pig in a secure area and keep away from them. Rabies is highly contractible to humans and is fatal.

Some countries, like the UK, are rabies free so vaccination will not be necessary here.

Pseudorabies (Aujeszky's disease)

Pseudorabies (PRV) is a highly contagious disease caused by a type of Herpes virus which is present in certain parts of the world, but has been eradicated, or is non-existent, in others.

It has been eradicated in the UK, and Denmark. There have been reported cases in Germany, Italy, Spain, Portugal and other parts of Europe. In Europe the disease is more commonly known as Aujeszky's disease rather than Pseudorabies.

If you live in the USA then it can possibly affect you depending on your state. In the USA certain states have a problem whilst in others it's non-existent. However, each state in the USA classifies the disease differently depending on how big of a problem it is for them.

Vaccination against the disease is a tricky issue. The problem is once a pig is vaccinated against the disease it will always test positive if an investigation or blood test is performed. This can mean a death sentence in certain states in the USA. Unless your state requires it, you shouldn't vaccinate against the disease. I highly recommend speaking with your vet about this and find out how this affects your state.

Also, when moving pigs in the USA you may be required to submit a blood test for PRV and Brucellosis. In certain states you may need to repeat these test 30 days after the original blood tests. It can also take a few days to obtain the necessary health certificates. All this will add extra time to your movement plan; make sure you factor this in to your plans.

If you live in Europe I would highly recommend speaking to your vet about this disease. Depending on where you live this may or may not affect you. There might be certain rules and regulations that you have to follow. So contact your vet and find out,

Worming

To correctly worm your pig you'll need to know their exact weight. This will allow you to calculate the correct dosage of wormer. If you aren't familiar with worming livestock it is a good idea to contact your vet and ask for advice.

There are three usual ways of administering worming drugs: orally, applied to the skin, or injected into the pig.

The easiest way for the novice to administer a wormer is to use Ivomec (Ivomectrin) injectable, and <u>feed</u> it to the pig orally. The injectable version of this drug <u>can</u> be administered through ingestion. To do this you need to:

Find out the exact weight of your pig.

Using the instructions that come with the Ivomec, calculate the correct dose. The rule of thumb is to <u>double the injectable dose when administering it orally.</u>

Hide the medicine in some food. I recommend using peanut butter, the drug can be mixed in and they're unlikely to notice there is any medication in there.

Most people use Ivomec 1% solution for pigs.

Don't inject your pigs unless you are 100% sure how to do it. If in doubt get a vet to perform the administration or stick to feeding it to them orally.

Most wormers will cover you against common internal parasites such as roundworm and lungworm. Certain brands of wormer can also have the added cover against external parasites such as mange (which is covered later).

Be sure to check the cover of the worming drug you are using. Different drugs cover different parasites, some drugs have a wider range of coverage than others. If you are unsure about this, contact your local livestock vet for professional advice about the subject.

Lameness

If your pig appears to be limping, or their feet seem painful, your pet might be lame. Pigs can become lame for a variety of reasons. These can include:

- Injury

- Poor diet

- Old age

- Poor hoof care

Pigs aren't the most sure-footed of animals, like humans they can slip and fall, and injure themselves. If this happens to your pig, confine them to a small flat area to prevent any further injury. You may need to minimise their movements for a few days to allow the injury to heal.

Aspirin can be used to relieve the worst of the pain – an adult pig can be given approximately 300mg twice daily to help alleviate any pain. The rule of thumb regarding dosage is 5mg per 1lb (5mg per 0.45kg). Aspirin can cause stomach problems, so make sure it's administered with a full meal to help prevent any potential problems. You should never feed a pig aspirin for more than a couple of days. Speak with the vet if you have any doubts.

Problems such as arthritis, rickets and poor bone development can occur in animals that have been fed a poor diet—one lacking in essential minerals and nutrients. Make sure you feed your pig sow nuts in the morning and some leafy dark greens in the afternoon. Nutritionally a diet like this will promote good all-round health, however their diet can be topped up with cod liver oil/powder, flax oil or a children's vitamin tablet—please see the Feeding section for more detail. Improving their diet may not solve lameness, but it could help alleviate some of their symptoms.

Obese pigs are more prone to lameness. Pigs' bones and muscles are designed to carry a certain amount of weight and no more. The additional weight carried by an obese pig places extra stress on the joints, muscles and bones. This results in more damage and lameness. Obese pigs are far more likely to develop severe arthritis, in old age, than a healthy pig. This highlights how important a good diet is, and why you should never overfeed your pig. If your pig is fat, put them on a diet and make them shed the extra weight—you could be looking at expensive vet's bills in future if you don't.

Older pigs are more prone to lameness and arthritis. Sadly, this is just something which accompanies old age. Diet is especially important as it can reduce some of the symptoms. Aspirin can be used to alleviate extreme cases of lameness and arthritis.

Rimadyl is one drug which is used to help lameness and arthritis in older pigs. This is a prescription drug in most countries so you'll have to contact your vet if you wish to obtain it. This drug can cause your pig to have a tummy upset so it needs to be taken with food, and something like Pepcid AC heartburn tablets (known as Pepcidtwo in other countries).

Make sure older animals are kept warm at night. Give them extra bedding, insulate their sty, essentially, do whatever it takes to make their sty and bed warm especially during the colder months. Cold weather and climates can make lameness worse.

Untrimmed hooves are also a major cause of lameness. Keep the hooves trimmed–make sure they're nice and neat. Untrimmed hooves will slowly stretch the tendons and place additional stress on the joints, if left untreated. For more details see the Hoof section later in this book.

Heat Stress and Sunburn

Pigs are susceptible to heat stress and sunburn. As a general rule pigs are comfortable in temperatures that humans are comfortable in.

On very warm days, or if you live in a warm climate, you will need to provide shade for your pig. Trees can provide them with shade; as can access to a cool building such as a barn or stable. If you have neither then you will have to build something for them. You cannot let them go without, it could kill them.

You should also provide your pig with some sort of wallow; a children's paddling pool, dug into the ground, makes an excellent wallow–just make sure the sides aren't too steep or high, the pig needs to be able to get in and out easily or they'll be reluctant to use it.

A simple wallow can be made by wetting an area of ground and creating a large, muddy puddle. Pigs do not need mud to wallow, they just need a cool pool of some sort. A muddy wallow does have the benefit of being better for their skin though. The mud helps prevent the pig from insect bites and sunburn, it also helps moisturise their skin.

Make your pig a wallow during the hot days–they will love you for it, trust me.

When a pig becomes too warm they will get heat stress. This is a very serious condition. A pig suffering from heat stress will usually be lying down panting. The panting will increase over time and, if left untreated, will result in the animal's death. If you suspect your pig is suffering heat stress it is critical that you help the pig cool down and try to reduce its temperature. First, you should try to get the pig out of the sun, if possible. If you cannot do this then wet it with cool water, or spray it with a hose pipe. Soaking absorbent fabric, such as towels, in water and placing them on the pig is another way to bring its temperature down. Make sure that the fabric doesn't dry out; they should <u>always</u> be full of water.

Always make sure your pig has access to fresh water. A lack of water on a warm day will increase the chance of heat stress happening. A lack of water will also cause salt poisoning as well.

Sunburn

Sunburn can be a problem on hot days. Usually most adult pigs have the common sense to keep themselves out of the hot sun, however young piglets, who are more prone to sunburn than older animals, may not be as smart.

If your pig develops sunburn you can treat this the same way as humans do–with calamine lotion or an after sun cream. Make sure that you move your animal out of the sun first, before treating them. Luckily pigs cannot lick most of their body, so you can safely apply creams without fear of them licking and ingesting them.

Pig oil is sometimes used on animals to prevent dry and flaky skin. It also helps maintain a healthy looking coat. Never apply pig oil to your animal on a hot day–it will fry them. Pig oil should be applied in the evenings, ideally before the pig retires to bed.

Pig Lice

Pig mites are long, grey/brown lice and can be seen by the naked eye. Below is a link to a few pictures of them:

http://goo.gl/ylltYf

They're usually found around the neck area and inside in the base of the ears.

Symptoms of an infestation include the pig shaking its head and sometimes holding its head to one side. Be sure to check regularly inside the pig's ears–signs of a mite infestation can result in the pig's ears containing a black paste.

Pig mites are easily treated with specialist washing solutions and mite powders, available from the vet. When using these treatments make sure you wash out the inside of their ears as well as any other affected areas.

Mange and Scabies

Pigs can suffer from two forms of mange: Sarcoptic and Demodectic.

Sarcoptic mange is the same type of mange which can affect dogs, cows, horses and other livestock. This type of mange is caused by a mite that burrows under the skin. Pigs affected by this usually have red patches and small pimples on their skin. Hair loss will also occur on the affected areas; this is usually through the pig frantically trying to scratch the affected parts. Lesions will typically appear on the legs, shoulders, belly, neck, ears and head. The affected parts may also start to bleed if left untreated and secondary bacterial infections often occur. Given enough time a pig can become weak from the effects of the mange.

Demodectic mange is the less contagious of the two and only affects pigs.

Both types of mange will produce an orange stain; look for symptoms on the belly, under the front legs, between the rear legs or behind the ears. The vet will need to take a skin sample to test for an infestation; they will examine the skin sample under a microscope to check for the presence of the tiny mites that cause mange.

Mange mites have a two-week life cycle. The usual way to treat a mange infestation is using Ivomec: two doses, two weeks apart. The first dose kills any mites living on the skin (but it won't kill their eggs); the second treatment, given two weeks later, will kill the newly hatched mites. In extreme cases a third dose can be given two weeks after the second dose.

For details on how to dose a pig with Ivomec see the Worming section.

A mange wash can also be used on the badly affected areas on a pig's skin. This will give the pig more immediate relief. This won't kill all the mites though, it should be used in conjunction with Ivomec.

Clean their home/sty and disinfect if necessary. Make sure you change their bedding. If you bed your pig down with blankets, or something similar, wash it in the washing machine on a 90° cycle.

Skin Care

Pigs can suffer from dry, flaky skin; this is especially visible on black pigs and Potbellies. Poor skin condition can be an indication that your pet is not being fed the correct diet so try feeding your pig more: dark, leafy, green vegetables; flax or cod liver oil or a children's vitamin tablet. Flaky skin is better being treated from the inside out. It may take a few weeks for their skin problem to improve. If a change in diet doesn't eliminate the problem, you can try pig oil.

Pig oil can also be applied once a week, to help eliminate flaky skin. Try to use a non-perfumed brand of pig oil. Also never let an oiled pig go outside during sunny weather, they will fry. Ideally, pig oil should be applied in the evenings before they go to bed. Please note that pig oil will only mask the problem, a change of diet is the best treatment for flaky skin.

Brushing a pig can also eliminate flaky skin; it's also great for removing loose hair. A horse brush, or something similar, is good for this. Frequent brushing will result in your pet developing a lovely coat in great condition. Bear in mind some pigs like brushing, others hate it.

Chapter 17 - Old Age Pigs (OAPs)

Once a pig reaches around ten years of age they are considered to be an OAP. Once they are fourteen they usually begin to develop health problems, such as: arthritis, declining vision, loss of hearing, loss of smell and tooth loss. Uterine tumours often claim the lives of un-spayed sows.

Once your pig reaches this age there are measures you can take to help alleviate some of the problems that come with old age. These are:

Make sure that your pig is a healthy weight. If your pig is on the heavy side it will make any arthritis worse–you may need to cut back slightly on their food – an arthritic pig is less active, and less active pigs need less food.

Make sure you keep their hooves trimmed. Misshapen hooves will make any arthritis worse. Overgrown pig hooves force the foot and ankles into awkward positions placing extra strain on the joints.

Give them a little extra warmth and softer bedding. Make sure their bed is comfortable and throw in an extra blanket or two, if needed, or extra straw. You don't want your pig to become overheated, but if you live in a cold climate a little extra warmth will help.

Make sure your arthritic pig avoids any stairs, even if they are used to them. If you can, cover any stairs with a non-slip ramp (rubber car mats are good for this), make sure they are not slippery when wet.

Start giving your pig a health supplement. This could be cod liver oil, flax oil, sea cucumber, Glucosamine or Chondroitin supplements. Some people have also reported success using equine arthritis vitamin supplements.

Rimadyl is a drug that can be obtained from veterinarians in some countries. This is a great treatment for pigs with arthritis. Make sure you give this drug with food as it can cause your pig to have a stomach upset. It might also be worth adding a Pepcid Antacid or something similar to the food–just to be on the safe side.

Switch the pig onto a different type of pellet once they reach their elder years. There are brands of pig pellet designed specifically for pigs in their senior years. It might be worth having a look on the Internet to try and find brands in your country.

Another point to be mindful of, when dealing with OAPs, is stress. Due to their age they may have a weak heart, so be careful when doing things likely to cause them a lot of stress. In extreme cases, severe stress can cause older animals to have a heart attack. Hoof trimming (especially if you have to roll your pig onto their backs or restrain them), moving your pig into a transport trucks or a cow trailer are examples of things which will cause a pig stress.

Another thing to watch out for, when dealing with older animals, is a sudden loss of appetite. Pigs may miss the occasional meal but if they refuse to eat for more than a few days call out the vet. If your pig does stop eating try tempting them with treats such as: yoghurt, cold porridge or peanut butter, if this doesn't work it could mean something is wrong.

Chapter 18 - Hoof Care

Pigs, just like sheep and goats, are cloven-hoofed animals. So it's necessary to trim their feet whenever the need arises.

If left untreated, overgrown hooves will cause ligament damage and an increased chance of severe arthritis later in life. Also, it places extra stress on the pig's bones and joints.

Hoof care for pigs can be a difficult job to do. A lot depends on how tame your pet is, and if they're used to you touching their feet. However, there are solutions to problem pigs and preventative measures you can take to help minimise the chances of hoof trimming being necessary. We shall discuss these later in the chapter.

If you're not comfortable with the idea of trimming your pig's feet then it might be worth getting the vet to show you how it's done.

Tools for the Job

Make sure you buy a good pair of hoof clippers that are nice and sharp. We usually use foot rot shears; however, I've known people use rose clippers, goat trimmers, sheep trimmers and horse trimmers. Don't buy cheap as pig hooves are notoriously tough and hard to cut, so make sure you buy the best quality tools for the job.

Secateurs can also be used on hooves; they have a long blade which can be used on a pig when it's standing. If your pigs don't like their hooves being trimmed then these can help. You can use them to snip the odd bit off when they're drinking or feeding.

A cordless Dremel type tool is also handy, to smooth cut edges and shape the hoof. Just be careful with these though as the sound of the tool can make pigs nervous–introducing it slowly over a period of time and hoof treatments should accustom them to the noise.

A horse hoof file, farriers' file and wood rasp file can all be used to smooth the cut edges and to shape the hoof as well.

Whatever tools you use make sure they're of good quality. Pig hooves are usually very hard and tough to cut. Hoof trimming can be distressing enough for owners and their pigs, so make sure you have a good pair of clippers that will allow you to complete the task as quickly as possible.

Hoof Care and Piglets

If you want to make regular hoof care easy, it's best to start training your pig when they're young. You need to get your pet accustomed to you touching their feet; you don't want them to panic when you start to use the hoof clippers on them.

To start foot training you should play with your piglet's feet, when they're lying down on their side. To start the training you should:

1. Scratch your piglet's belly to try to make them fall onto their side.

2. Once down, start touching the feet.

3. Gently pick up the hooves and move them around slightly – try to replicate the motions that you might use when performing a trim.

4. If piggy becomes nervous just go back to scratching the belly and leave the feet alone for a little while, once they're comfortable again just repeat the process of touching their hooves.

5. After a few days or weeks of this, they will have become used to you touching their hooves. Once this has happened, you'll need to get your pig used to the sensation of the hoof clippers.

6. While your pig is lying down and letting you play with its feet, just try touching their hoof with the clippers. Try scraping the clippers gently against their hoof, you can also try nipping the tips (you're not aiming to remove anything from the hoof, at this stage, you are simply introducing your pig to the sensation).

When performing training like this it's a good idea to talk to your pig in a reassuring and calm manner throughout. This will help to keep them calm and let them know they're being good. Once you are finished give them a little bit of a treat for being well-behaved.

Training your piglet in this way makes hoof care a lot easier. You will really appreciate this once your pig is fully grown. You can still train tame adult pigs to get used to the sensation of hoof trimming, however the process usually takes a bit longer.

When it comes to this sort of training, some pigs will tolerate it, others won't. Only time will tell which one yours is, and whether he'll be happy to have his feet trimmed without restraint.

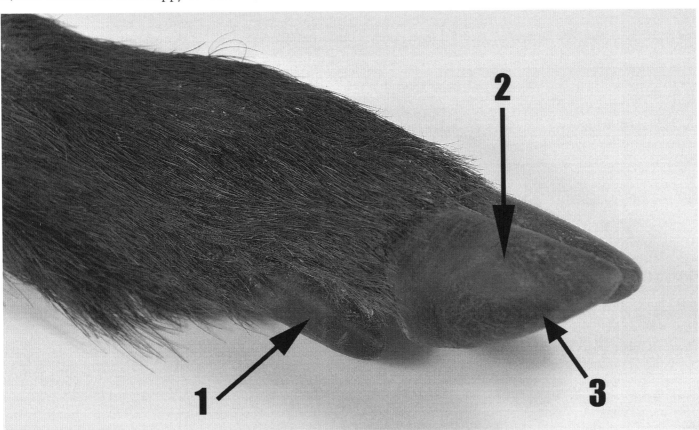

How to Trim your Pig's Feet

The above picture is of a pig's hoof. This consists of:

1. Two dewclaws at the back of the hoof.

2. Two toes at the front of the hoof with a hard nail surrounding each toe.

3. Blood vessels, similar to the quick in human nails. You cannot see this in the picture, but if you started to trim the hoof you would see it in this approximate position. It runs around the base of the hoof a few millimetres away from the tip in this picture.

The main hooves (toes) will need reducing in length and trimming. The trick is to snip only small slices off at a time, gradually reducing the excess length. The hoof should be trimmed back until it is well rounded. It should then be finished and shaped with a flat file. The excess ends of your pig's hoof may be the most difficult to cut as they'll be dry and embedded with dirt, they can be quite tough to chop.

The nerve in a pig's foot extends further into the hoof than the blood vessels; therefore you're more likely to hit this before you cause any bleeding. If your pig starts to moan this could mean you've hit the nerve, stop trimming immediately if this is the case. If you do cause bleeding apply antiseptic foot spray, this should help the hoof clot and prevent any further bleeding.

The dewclaws are the next to be trimmed; they need to be altered and shortened. They will also need to be smoothed with a file. There are nerves and blood vessels in this part of the pig hoof, so be careful not to clip too much off.

Hoof moisturiser can be applied, to help prevent any splits and cracks appearing in the hoof. Hoof moisturiser for horses can be used on pigs if you are struggling to find a dedicated pig hoof treatment.

It's worth noting that you do not have to try cutting all four hooves in one go. If it takes you a few weeks to successfully cut all four hooves then that's fine. Hoof trimming should be performed on your pig approximately every 1-1.5 years–if takes a month or two to finish the job that is fine.

Clipping a fully grown pig's hooves can sometimes be a difficult process, especially if they are not tame. We will talk about some possible solutions to this problem next.

Problem Pigs and Untamed Animals

Some pigs do not like to have their hooves trimmed, other pigs might not be tame enough to allow you to clip them. There are a few possible solutions to such problems:

The Rolling Technique

Sitting your pig on his rump against you is one solution–this is easier said than done.

The trick is to get them in this position as quickly as possible.

You need to quickly lift the pig's front end and roll them back onto their rump. You can then either: sit them on their rump with their back against you, or roll them completely onto their backs. Sometimes it helps to fall back with the pig and sit down with the pig between your legs.

The main aim of this technique is to try and get the pig's feet off the floor as quickly as possible. You need to stop the pig from being able to gain leverage and scramble away.

Personally I find that this is a job for two people. It can sometimes take a few attempts to manoeuvre the pig into the right position. You might also have to wait for your pet to calm down after making a failed attempt. Patience is the key when doing this.

Also, wear your ear plugs. They will scream the place down when they're placed on their backs. But it gets the job done.

Here are two excellent videos which illustrates this technique:

http://vimeo.com/1158543

http://www.youtube.com/watch?v=R92y52vkXQ8

Be careful when trying this technique with old animals. Old pigs are more prone to becoming highly stressed if you're trying to turn them over and manhandle them into place. You run the possible risk of heart attack or physical damage, due to the force required during this procedure. When it comes to older pigs, who are uncooperative about their hoof trimming, preventative measures are sometimes the best course of action and we will discuss those at the end of this chapter.

Sedation

For very problematic animals things get a little trickier. Sedation can be used on animals which are not tame or are very uncooperative. Before sedating any pig make sure you discuss the problem with your vet, they may be able to provide you with an alternative.

There are risks involved when sedating pigs. If your animal is old or overweight then the risk of injury and death during sedation, goes up. The age and weight of your pig are important factors you must inform your vet about when consulting them about sedation.

If you ever sedate a pig at home make sure you remove them from the rest of the herd. If the herd see the sedated pig acting strangely and appearing weak, they may attack it (to establish their dominance over it). Likewise, you should never place a pig back into the herd until it's recovered 100% from the sedation, or you risk the same.

Tilt Table/Pig Slings

Restraining the pig during hoof clipping can be a challenge. As mentioned previously the trick is to get their feet off the floor, otherwise you don't stand a chance of being able to trim them. One option, for the DIY inclined, might be to build a pig sling. Such devices are used in laboratories, vets, and in the meat pig industry. They are very expensive to buy but alternatives can be built. For more information try searching the Internet for the term 'pig sling' or 'panepinto sling'.

Here's a link to a few pictures of pig slings:

http://goo.gl/gGHSWh

This will give you an idea of the type of device you might choose to build, if you felt capable of doing so. The aim of such devices is to elevate your pig a few inches off the ground, comfortably.

I've seen a DIY pig sling fashioned out of a large piece of canvas with four <u>feet</u>-holes cut into it. The pig was then restrained whilst the sling was moved under them. It then took 2-4 people to lift the piggy off the ground, and another to clip the feet whilst it was restrained.

Remember you could hurt your animal using such a contraption. My advice would be that you do not attempt to make such a device unless you are 100% confident in your DIY skills. I have included this information for reference purposes only. It is by no means endorsing your decision to build your own, if you have a problem piggy then it may be worth the investment of buying a sling as you may need to use it again.

Pig Chutes and Tilt Tables

Another method of restraining pigs is to use a pig chute or tilt table. These are more commonly used with livestock such as sheep, goats and young calves. Here's a link to a few images of these devices:

http://goo.gl/eFfmTH

These devices have a gate at either end. The animal is walked in, and then confined in the middle, using gates. The middle section of the device is then tightened around the animal to firmly hold them in place. Once the animal is secure the middle section of the device can be rotated 90°, lifting the animal onto its side. The hooves can now be easily trimmed without having to break your back trying to turn the pig over. When finished, you simply roll the table back to its starting position and release the animal via the gate.

These devices are expensive and are probably a bit much for your average pet pig owner. But, if you plan to keep a few pigs, they could be very handy.

These devices are commonly used by the larger vet surgeries and those which have to deal with a lot of livestock.

Preventative Tips For Hoof Care

A great way to minimise the necessity for hoof trimming is to run your pig on a mixture of hard and soft ground—this will naturally wear away their hooves.

If you have a concrete, or paved, area on your property you could try feeding your pig on it. You could also surround their water point with paving stones, roofing felt, concrete or another hard, abrasive surface. Similarly you could place a hard/abrasive surface before the entrance to their sty or bed.

Whatever you use your pig will have to be on it daily, for at least a few minutes. This solution will not resolve all of your hoof trimming problems but they may reduce the frequency of trimming.

Chapter 19 - Breeding pigs

You need to think hard and long about whether you want to breed pet pigs, it is not a decision to be made lightly. Breeding any livestock is hard work; it also requires a significant investment of time and money.

When breeding livestock, things can go badly wrong, especially if you lack experience. Pigs can die when they give birth, sows can produce stillborn piglets, sows can also accidentally stand on and crush their piglets; inadvertently killing them. This is just a small sample of the problems you face when breeding pigs.

You need to have the capability to deal with things like this when breeding animals, it certainly isn't for the faint of heart. A good breeder knows how to reduce the risks through experience, careful selection of breeding animals and having the right setup and equipment.

Before you consider breeding pigs you need to ask yourself this question: 'What will I do if I cannot sell the piglets I produce?' I wish more people would ask themselves this question before they decide to breed pigs. I've lost count of the number of people who've contacted me to offer piglets that they cannot sell.

People have often been lured into breeding pet pigs (especially Micro Pigs in recent years) thinking that it's a 'get rich quick' scheme and easy money. They often hear the rumours about piglets selling for expensive prices and they think it'll be easy for them to do the same.

Likewise people often rush into pig breeding without doing any market research. You need to examine your local area and ask yourself: how much competition do I have? Look at various local classified advertising mediums, note how many sellers you are up against, and the average price their piglets are making. Market research for any business is vitally important, only a fool starts a business without looking into these things.

The reality of the situation is far different, for example, the average price of Micro Pigs in the UK are now similar to their Kune Kune and Potbellied Pig counterparts. There are a few breeders out there still commanding high prices, but these are breeders who've built up and established their business, and their reputation, over time. If you're new to breeding pigs and you plan to sell yours through classified ads, or something similar, then you might find you struggle to achieve the prices you want. You may even end up selling them at a loss.

The trouble with selling pigs through classified advertising, and other similar mediums, is that everyone else has also had the same idea. Your prices will have to be competitive against the other sellers, unless you offer something different. It's not easy selling pigs solely via classified adverts, and it is very easy to be left with animals you cannot sell. This is why you need to seriously think long and hard before you consider breeding pigs commercially or as a hobby.

Please try to be a good breeder, one who is responsible for the pigs they sell. Don't lie about your pigs to make a fast bit of money, or sell to people who cannot realistically keep them well. If you do then your pigs have every chance of ending up in the sanctuaries, which are already full to the brim, or they risk simply being abandoned.

If you are still set on wanting to breed pigs then I advise you to contact your local vet to discuss the idea and gain some professional advice on the subject and an understanding of the commitment and costs involved.

Please note that this section is not a comprehensive guide to breeding. It is designed just to cover basic pig breeding. I suggest that you read up on the subject as much as possible before committing to anything.

Unexpected Pregnancies

Over the years a lot of people have contacted me for advice on how to deal with unexpected pregnancies. These unlucky people have been given (or rescued) a pig, only to have it give birth a few months, or even weeks, later. The people I helped had never bred pigs before so they were completely unprepared for the experience.

If this happens to you please use the information in this section to help you through the process. If you need any additional advice feel free to contact me at info@lancashiremicropigs.co.uk.

Selecting Animals

Only the best quality animals should be picked for breeding. If you are buying your animals then you should purchase the best genes you can afford. Never breed sickly or ill pigs.

How many pigs should you buy for breeding? I would personally recommend that you start off small, maybe two sows and one boar. On average, this would produce a litter every six months, giving you plenty of time to sell your piglets before the next litter arrives.

The boar is the most important member of your breeding herd. He's 50% of the genes of your herd. A good boar can make up for a lack of quality genes in your sows. This is part of the reason why some breeders opt for artificial insemination, as this allows them to use great genes without the added cost of keeping a male.

Sows should be at least twelve months old before being used to breed. Pay close attention to their health during the first year of their life, if you're having to deal with health problems, injuries, lameness, etc. then select another pig for breeding. You do not want to pass these traits onto your piglets.

If you are planning to have your sow served by someone else's boar, make sure you do your homework. Ideally you want to use a proven boar with a good history behind him. There is nothing wrong with asking the owner of the boar to provide this information.

When it comes to serving pigs, take the sow to the boar, not the other way around. The sow should be left with the boar for at least a month if she's to become pregnant.

Artificial insemination is often popular with smaller breeders, so they do not have to keep a boar themselves, or take their gilts elsewhere to be served. Some artificial insemination services offer the best quality sperm from the top breeding stock in their country or even the world. This is a great way to ensure that only the very best genes are used in your pig breeding.

With the exception of Micro Pigs, pedigree systems are in place for other breeds such as the Kune Kune and Pot-bellied Pigs. This provides a degree of traceability of the genes in these breeds; it also helps to qualify the genes you are using. To my knowledge there are no pedigree systems in place for Micro Pigs.

Getting Setup

If you intend to breed your pigs you may need to set up your premises and pigs' area differently.

You need to setup an area where your female pig can give birth and raise her young—this is called a farrowing area. This area needs to be sealed off from the rest of your herd so she can take care of her piglets safely.

Any boars you have on-site should be kept separate and fenced off from the females—unless you want regular pregnancies to occur. Keep the boars separate from the females so you can time the arrival of litters better – it's always best to try and have piglets born a few weeks before the busiest parts of the year (i.e. spring and summer months). You should also avoid having a litter in the middle of winter when trade might be a bit quiet.

When timing the arrival of your pig's litter you need to remember that the piglets will need to be fully weaned before they'll be ready to move to their new homes. This takes a minimum of 6-10 weeks so be sure to factor this additional time in to your plans.

If you are planning to keep a boar on site you might need to modify your fencing. An un-castrated boar will try to get through any fencing, put up between him and any female, especially when the sows come into season. You'll need to make sure that your fencing is <u>very</u> secure. Personally, I tend to reinforce any static fencing with an electric fence to keep gilts and boars apart. A single strand of electric fencing is a great way to stop a randy boar from destroying your fencing when he's trying to reach a female.

The Sow

Sows will come into season approximately every three weeks, this is called hogging. The hogging will last anything up to 72 hours (approximately three days). There are various signs and indicators that your pig is in season (or hogging) these can include:

- A change in behaviour – they may become whiny, noisy, and aggressive.

- Their vulva may become swollen; there might also be a slight discharge from it.

- They will become more tolerant to your touch. If you place a hand on their back they may stand still as if presenting themselves to you.

- They will be attracted to, or they'll want to reach, any boars you have on your site.

- Your boar will also be excited and agitated; they might foam at the mouth. They will be able to smell the pheromones being produced by the female and this will cause them to become excited.

- The other sows in the herd might start jumping on the hogging sow's back.

- Once your sow is hogging you should place them with the boar and leave them together for a month. If the sow does not come into heat toward the end of that month then you can be sure she has been inseminated. Make a note of the time and date, this will allow you to plan when your piglets are due to arrive. A pig's gestation period is approximately three months, three weeks and three days.

Your female can be left with the boar until she's ready for farrowing, 2-4 weeks before she's due, move her to the farrowing area that you have created.

The Farrowing Area

A farrowing area needs to be created at your site. As mentioned previously this area should be separate from your existing herd, as the sow needs to be able to rear her pigs in safety.

Pigs can farrow outside in a sty if the weather's not too cold. To test this take a temperature reading in the sow's sty or farrowing area. The ideal nest temperature is 35-40° Celsius. You need to take a reading with her in the nest as her body heat will warm the sty or room up. If the weather is cold a dedicated farrowing room is recommended. On our farm we use a room in a barn that we converted specifically for this purpose. We replaced the windows and doors in the room (to ensure it's as draught free as possible) and fitted a watering system and gates to the room.

Using a well-equipped room like this allows us to farrow litters during very cold winters as the room is weather proof and warm.

The gates in the room are used to separate the sow from her piglets–there are various times you'll need to do this: when you weigh your piglets, when giving them any medication, or even getting them ready for castration. Make sure your gating system is secure because your sow will try to destroy it when you start removing her young.

The farrowing pen should be flat and not have any large steps in it. The sow's belly will balloon during the last few weeks of pregnancy; it's not uncommon for it to scrape on the floor, especially for breeds like the Potbelly. Any steps in the room might rub and catch the sow's teats during the latter weeks of the pregnancy. This could cause them to become sore and painful.

Photo above: Sow in her nest in a farrowing pen - a sow will balloon in size during the last few weeks of pregnancy

Nesting Area

You need to provide your sow with a nesting area where she can give birth. This will be her bedding area and where she will give birth in the farrow pen. This could be in the sty or shed if you are farrowing outside. As a rule of thumb her nesting area wants to be approximately 8'x8'. A pen smaller than this size will increase the chances of the sow crushing her piglets once they are born.

Extra straw should be added to her bed/nest area. Be careful not to add too much, as newborn piglets can become trapped inside it. If the piglets are trapped in the excess straw, they sometimes cannot move out of the way of the sow when she lays down—this can result in piglets becoming crushed or smothered. The ideal temperature for the sow's nest is between 35-40° Celsius. Place a thermometer at floor level to correctly take a reading.

Some breeders place a low roof in the sow's nesting area. This will cause the nest to become warmer than the rest of the room. You can also add extra insulation to the roof if needed. The sow alone will produce plenty of body heat to keep her piglets warm, if you can trap this then you'll reduce the chances of you needing to use heat lamps or other electrical heaters in the farrowing pen.

Try to make sure the nesting area is well lit and bright. Newborn piglets are attracted to the light and warmth. Make sure the nesting area is the brightest bit of the farrowing pen on the day of the birth; otherwise your newborn piglets could escape the nest and die from the cold (hypothermia). If you cannot do this make sure your piglets are trapped inside the nest but still allow the sow to get out – place a board of wood a few inches high at the entrance to the nest. This board needs to be tall enough to keep the newborn piglets inside the nest/sty/shed.

Bringing the Sow in to Farrow

With our own pigs we tend to move them to the farrowing room a month before they're due to give birth. During the last four weeks of pregnancy we double their daily feed, and feed the sows twice daily. I'm a big fan of adding cod-liver oil powder to their feed before they're due to give birth, I've heard that feeding it at least a month before your piglets are due helps the development of the unborn piglets in the womb.

Boredom can be a problem for the sow when confining her to the farrowing area. With our own pigs we tend to give them a snak-a-ball (feed ball discussed earlier in the Boredom section of this book), containing part of their daily ration of food. This provides the sow with something to do whilst they're farrowing, it's also a nice bit of exercise for them.

I'm also a big fan of setting up a feeding rack and filling it with silage or hay every day—this gives them something to chew on and helps keep them occupied.

The sow will be more tolerant of confinement in a small space during the latter stages of pregnancy. She will grow substantially in size, and she won't want to move around much.

Two weeks before she is due to give birth it is a good idea to inject the sow with the appropriate dosage of one of the following;- Ivomec, Dectomax, or Panomec. The sow will pass on these drugs to her unborn piglets via the placenta. Therefore the piglets will be immunised against worms and external parasites when they are born. This immunity will cover the piglets for the first 3-4 weeks of their lives so they will need to be immunised again after this period.

A heat lamp can be used if you are farrowing during the colder months or in a cold climate. Heat lamps are a real fire risk so make sure you set yours up correctly and safely. Incorrectly setup heat lamps can also burn the animals. In some USA states heat lamps are illegal so you may have to find an alternative. Never use an electric heat mat with a pig, they are prone to chewing and could electrocute themselves on it.

Please note that we do not take any responsibility for damage or accidents caused by heat lamps. Use your common sense when setting them up and follow the manufacturer's instructions when using one. Employ a professional electrician to fit yours if needed. You use them at your own risk.

The sow will start to build a nest approximately 2-3 days prior to the birth. She will start to drag straw, grass, silage, hay, dock leaves or anything else she can find, into her bed to make a nest. I had one sow drag, and rip up, half a dozen fabric sacks in her sty to make a nest. They really will use anything during this period. A great test to see if your pig is nesting and getting ready to give birth is to feed them some straw. If they take it in their mouth and carry it straight to the sty/bed, there's a good chance your sow is nesting and preparing to give birth.

The Birth

The sow will start to produce milk approximately 24 hours before she's due to give birth. To check you squeeze her teats when she's lying down—hold one at the base and squeeze as you pull it towards you (you're trying to simulate how a piglet would suck on it). If it produces milk, or a watery fluid, then you can be pretty sure she's not far off.

When the sow gives birth you have two options:

1. You can leave the sow in her nest/farrowing area and let nature take its course.

2. Help the sow through the birth. She could take anything up to ten hours to complete the birth, so you could be in for a long day or night.

Helping a Sow Give Birth

If you are accompanying your sow throughout the process you need to stay calm and quiet. Don't interfere too much.

When piglets are born you simply want to wipe them down with a towel and clean off some of the afterbirth, and then place them on a teat. Newborn piglets are pretty smart and they'll start to suckle straight away—they usually need no encouragement.

Be sure to wipe any afterbirth off their nose and mouth, to prevent any blockage in their airway. If you find a piglet has an excess of mucus around their head it is a good idea to place your little finger in their mouth to clear any blockage which might restrict their breathing.

Newborn piglets should easily be able to find their way to the teat without any help. They're born with their eyes open and they are able to move. They have a natural instinct to seek out the teat immediately, and they're usually pretty good at doing so.

The sow usually delivers approximately half her piglets lying on one side, she will then proceed to lie down on her other side and deliver the remaining piglets from her womb. Pigs need to turn over during the birthing process as their womb is in two parts.

If you have a piglet which is not breathing you need to make sure that the nose and mouth are not restricted by any mucus. You should then hold the piglet upside down for five minutes. Do **not** swing the piglet around as one might do with a newborn lamb.

Runts and stillborn piglets are common in most litters. The rate at which these happen depends on many factors. A large amount of stillborn piglets may be the result of poor genes, pig selection, diet or disease. This is why it's of the utmost importance that you get as much of the breeding process right before the pregnancy and subsequent birth. Doing so will help to reduce your mortality rates.

Post Birth

It's essential that the piglets get their mother's milk in the first 48 hours after they've been born. The mother's milk contains colostrum during this period, this needs to be passed onto the piglets. Colostrum contains important antibodies that need to be passed on to the newborns. When piglets are born they have no natural immunity, the antibodies in the colostrum provides this. Also, the colostrum is more readily absorbed during the first 24 hours of the piglet's life.

The sow should expel the afterbirth after the last piglet has been born. If your sow doesn't expel any afterbirth within a few hours after the last piglet, call the vet. It's not uncommon for the afterbirth, and possibly dead piglets, to sometime remain stuck in the womb. If left it will cause an infection and may have to be manually removed. If you are not comfortable with this get the vet to do it.

When the sow has expelled the afterbirth, clean it up and remove it, and add a little extra straw if needed. You should also remove any dead piglets which have been produced.

If everything goes well, you should now have a contented sow with her piglets happily suckling on her teats. A good sign is that the sow will grunt rhythmically and happily.

The sow should still be fed twice a day with a double ration of sow nuts. It's absolutely critical that she has a constant supply of water available. When constructing a farrowing pen I am more likely to fit a permanent water bowl that is plumbed into the water mains, as opposed to using the tyre/bucket method, discussed earlier in the book. This ensures that the sow has a constant supply of water and there's little chance of her running out. She will need the extra water to aid her with milk production. I personally also like to set up a hay rack and fill it every day with some silage/haylage/hay–I believe that this also aids milk production.

The first five days are probably the most critical in the lives of the piglets. If any problems are going to happen they're more likely to happen during this period. During this time the piglets are still a bit slow and docile, which makes them more susceptible to being crushed when the sow lies down. Some sows are better mothers than others, and some are more prone to crushing their piglets than others. Time will tell whether you have a good or bad mother. Good breeding pigs, which consistently produce healthy litters with low mortality rates, are to be treasured. Good sows get better with age due to the experience they accumulate.

After the first week or so we discontinue the use of any heat lamps. Obviously if you live in colder climates you may need to alter this.

During farrowing you need to keep an eye on your sow and her litter. Check her teats regularly and look for any signs of mastitis. It's not unknown for mastitis to develop in the first three days of the farrowing. Her udder will become hot, red and painful. Her milk supply may start to dwindle and she may become distressed. Do not take the piglets away from her. If this happens call a vet for the correct advice on how to deal with it. The usual method is to inject the sow with the appropriate dose of Oxytocin. The Oxytocin will encourage the sow to let down more milk. The vet maybe able to provide an antibiotic to help treat the mastitis.

During this process the piglets may need to be fed manually; human baby milk powder (diluted) can be used, but goat milk replacement is probably the best choice. If the piglets are under three days old you may need to feed them the replacement manually–feed them using a shallow dish of milk or individually using a bottle.

Be very careful when bottle feeding young pigs, it's very easy for them to aspirate–bottle feeding can push the liquid down into their lungs. I would personally try to feed them via the dish first before resorting to the bottle. Even day-old piglets have the intelligence to drink warm milk from a dish when they're hungry.

During the first few weeks you need to keep a close watch on your piglets. You're looking for sickly animals, and any presence of scour. Scour is where the young piglet's intestine is overwhelmed by pathogenic bacteria such as E. coli. If any piglets start to scour they will have dirty bottoms and diarrhoea (scour). Scour needs to be treated as soon as possible, it will affect their growth and nutrient intake; left untreated the piglets can eventually die. Scour treatments are easily obtained from the vet or agricultural suppliers.

- When dealing with scour preventative measures are the best course of action. These can include:

- Ensure the sow is producing milk. Check her teats, especially during the first 48 hours post-birth, when the piglets need the colostrum.

- Make sure the farrowing pen is clean, dry and free from draughts. This will help minimize the spread of harmful bacteria.

- Wash your hands before and after handling any piglets. Also wash your boots before entering the farrowing area.

- Remove any muck or faeces daily, and cover areas with clean sawdust after removal.

The aim of these steps is to minimize the spread and reproduction of any bacteria which may cause scour, or make it worse.

The First Two Weeks

By two weeks of age the piglets should start to take an interest in their mother's dry feed. By six weeks they should be eating part of their mother's dry feed. You will need to increase the sow's daily feed to accommodate these extra mouths.

If your pig is kept inside it's a good idea that when your piglets are approximately three weeks old you should start to throw the occasional sod of earth into the far end of the farrowing pen. This will provide the pig's diet with essential iron, which helps to promote healthy growth. If your piglets are farrowed outside then this is not a problem, they'll pick up the iron they need from the surrounding earth.

Alternatively, an iron injection, or oral supplement, can be given to pigs which are kept inside. Consult your vet about this as an incorrect dosage can be toxic. Personally, I find it easier just to keep throwing pieces of earth into their pen every few days rather than having to deal with injections or oral supplements.

During this time you want to start to socialise your piglets. They need to get used to humans if they are ever going make good pets. Try sitting in the pen with the piglets when they are feeding, they'll be curious about you and they'll come to investigate. Try talking to them and touching them, they'll be jumpy at first and the mother might be protective, but they need to get used to you. Once you can touch them, try to scratch them or a give them a belly rub, they'll love this—once you can do this to your piglets they are socialised properly. Try to sit in with them for 5-10 minutes a day, it may take a week or two for them to become tame but the results are worth it.

Castration

Castration should be performed on any boars which are destined to become pets. As discussed earlier in the book an un-castrated boar is a bad pet. Castration should be performed on any piglets between 2-5 weeks of age.

The process is preferably done sooner rather than later as this will promote the wound to heal better.

Castration has been routinely performed on pigs without the use of an anaesthetic, especially when young. Personally, when it comes castrating piglets, I prefer the operation to be done with the use of an anaesthetic and a sedative. With our own piglets we take them to the veterinarian surgery where they use an anaesthetic and a sedative to perform the operation.

Potbellied Pigs and Micro Pigs are susceptible to hernias when castration is performed, and these can be deadly. Also, the castration wound must have the inguinal loop stitch, closed. These are points only an experienced vet knows about, and knows how to prevent. Make sure you do the right thing and take your piglets to the surgery for castration. Don't do things on the cheap and castrate them at your home as you're risking their lives.

Weaning

The weaning should be finished at approximately 8-10 weeks of age. The exact time depends on how many piglets are with the sow, how they've put on weight, and their physical appearance. Don't try weaning your pigs too early as this can cause behavioural problems which might not appear until later in life.

After 8-10 weeks the sow should be removed from the piglets and placed back into the establish herd (this is called a 'drying period' or 'drying out'). The sow will fight with the established herd as they need to re-establish the pecking order. So it might be worth applying some Vaseline to her ears and providing her with some alternative sleeping quarters for the first few days.

Personally I tend to stick the heat lamp back on the piglets for the first few days after removal of the sow. This is to help the piglets overcome the stress of the sow's removal and will keep them a little warmer at night. Care needs to be taken when adding the sow back to the establish herd.

Bear in mind that the sow will want to get back to her piglets, so she'll be noisy, distressed and agitated during the first few days after her removal. She may also chew and attack fencing, gates and other things in her pen. If this is a problem you may have to use electric fencing to minimise the damage. After a few days this behaviour usually fades away.

If you're keeping any boars back for breeding, they should not be castrated. However, once the weaning is finished these un-castrated boars need to be removed and separated from any females and barrows (castrated males). Un-castrated adolescent boars are aggressive and uncontrollable. I have routinely seen them bully their female and barrow counterparts. This can affect food intake as they will dominate the rest of the herd and eat all the food. Separation should occur when they are around three months of age. This will also prevent any unwanted pregnancies occurring, as young boars are sexually active as early as three months old. Usually the only thing that prevents them from impregnating their mothers at this age is their size (they cannot mount her properly due to the height difference).

A few days after the sow has been removed the piglets are then ready to be sold or moved to new homes. It is a good idea to administer injections to the piglets once the sow is no longer present. We usually inject our piglets with the appropriate dosage of Ivomec, Panomec, Dectomax, etc., before they leave our farm. This ensures that they are free from parasites and also reduces the risk of carrying anything to their new homes.

Make sure that when you move your pigs, to their new home, you follow the necessary legal procedure and guidelines required by your country. See the Moving Pigs section for more details.

Chapter 20 - Conclusion

Congratulations on reaching the end of our guide. We hope you've enjoyed it and found it educational. You should now have a clearer idea of what a Micro Pig is, what alternatives there are, and (most importantly) how to take care of a pet pig properly.

Please feel free to join us @ Lancashiremicropigs.co.uk where we post monthly articles about pet pigs and their care.

Thanks and take care

Yours Sincerely

Joanne Rowe

Chapter 21 - Useful Sites and Links

Here's a list of UK and USA based links that you may find useful:

Sanctuaries

I urge anyone thinking of owning a pig to consider adopting one from a sanctuary first. Most of them are full to the brim and they need all the help they can get.

- http://www.Potbelliedpigs.co.uk/–The only dedicated UK based sanctuary.

- http://www.pigplacementnetwork.org/–USA.

- http://www.petfinder.com/–USA based search engine for rescue animals, includes pigs.

There are hundreds of other USA based pig sanctuaries. Use the link below to find them:

- http://goo.gl/dsi8PK

Useful Video links

- http://vimeo.com/1158543–hoof trimming video.

- http://www.youtube.com/watch?v=R92y52vkXQ8–feet trimming video.

- http://vimeo.com/12254342–tusk trimming video.

Further Reading

These useful sites are worth bookmarking:

- http://www.britishkunekunesociety.org.uk/–UK Kune Kune site, good forum and plenty of advice about the breed.

- http://www.petpigs.com/–North American Potbellied Pig Association.

- http://goo.gl/O2zhYu–Yahoo group setup by the late Pris Valentine. Very active board, even today in 2014. If you want to chat about pet pigs this is the place to go. A wealth of experience in this group.

- http://www.farec.org/pigs.htm–USA based sanctuary. Has loads of great information.

- http://www.pigpalssanctuary.com/health/health_care_articles.htm–Sadly this sanctuary is closed. However they have left their website up for information purposes.

- http://en.allexperts.com/q/Potbellied-Pigs-3478/–Q&A site for pet pig owners.

- http://lancashiremicropigs.co.uk/-Our own website. We no longer sell pigs but do provide information and guides on their care.

Like this Book, Please Leave a Review

If you like this book can you please consider leaving a review on Amazon.

Reviews really help us and they help to show others how useful this book really is.

You can find this book's kindle page by using any of the links below:

- http://www.amazon.com/dp/B00H52F4KW–USA Link

- https://www.amazon.co.uk/dp/B00H52F4KW–UK Link

And you can find this book's page by typing the ISDN number into the Amazon search bar. The ISDN number is:

ISBN-13: 978-1494824501

Thanks for that. It's really appreciated

Kind regards

Joanne Rowe

Index